Praise for Lin⟨
(and 52 Other Re-Told Childhood Tales)

Delightful! An inspiring, touching, and oftentimes humorous look at family life in small-town Mississippi. Through the wonder of story, **Lines in the Gravel** *reminds us of the importance of passing along to the next generation those values that have blessed us and shaped us for good. Whether you grew up in a warm and loving family or a highly dysfunctional family, you'll be better for having read this book!*

Stan Buckley,
Executive Director, But God Ministries

"The places of our childhood may have been different, but I recognized a common thread between Al Ainsworth's stories in **Lines in the Gravel (and 52 Other Re-Told Childhood Tales)** *and those from my own childhood. The same values of faith and family that I learned growing up in rural Mississippi continue to be the values that guide me as the leader of my own home and as the leader of young men today. Al reminds us all to express our values of faith and family through the stories that we tell."*

Hugh Freeze
Head Football Coach, University of Mississippi

"Growing up in the South Mississippi family that I did, sports and stories were constant companions. The sport or the level at which it was being played didn't matter. Much of what it took for me to have success in the NFL can be traced back to games all over South Mississippi and the conversations that happened in the Favre household afterward. **Lines in the Gravel (and 52 Other Re-Told Childhood Tales)** *reminds us of the value of our stories to shape who we are and who we aspire to be."*

Brett Favre, Three-Time National Football League MVP

Lines in the Gravel
(and 52 Other Re-Told Childhood Tales)

AL AINSWORTH

Cover by Leighton Dees

Cover Photo by Charlie Plyler

DEDICATION

This book is dedicated to all the people who influenced me in my childhood years (up until about age 19, the period of my life that this book covers). You are still very much a part of who I am today. Particularly, this book is dedicated to my family of origin, whom I now fondly call my Lines in the Gravel family. In more ways than the obvious reasons, I couldn't have done this without you. I love you all.

CONTENTS

Acknowledgments   xi

Foreword by Walt Grayson   xiii

Introduction   1

1   Meet the Family   6

2   That Darned Ol' Happy Man and His Samuncrium   9

3   We're a Competitive Lot   12

4   Wilagene: Bless Her Heart   15

5   Star Proper   18

6   A Black Welcome Mat and My Inheritance   20

7   Family Names, Southern Names   22

8   The Store (or The De-Flagpoling of Edward Bone)   24

9   How Granny Came To Be Called Granny   27

10 Ah and Ee (and the Tragic Convertible Accident That Cost Them Their   3
Lives"

11 Still Sittin' Here When I Get Back!   32

12 When Pop Came Down   36

13 Yucky Water and the Grumps   38

14 A Most Unusual Crop   41

15 One Thousand Laps Around the Carport   44

16 Goodies with Granny   46

17	Lines in the Gravel	49
18	Andy and the Book Satchel	51
19	Smokie, the Successful Chaser of Cars	54
20	Corn Flakes at Midnight	57
21	The Uninhibited Joy of a Romp in the Mud	60
22	Church Adventures	62
23	Teddy and the Hot Dog	67
24	Devil in the Ditch	70
25	Dad's Motorcycle and a Bet with the Preacher	73
26	Twenty-Five Red Christmas Ribbons (or Lines in the Gravel Revisited)	75
27	A Cup of Coffee with My Mama	78
28	Mama Bluebird	82
29	The Price of Boiled Peanuts	85
30	Gardenias and Perker	87
31	When Stacy Dilmore Pitched, We Had a Chance	90
32	Jock	93
33	The Howling Kid at the Baptist Church	96
34	Chubs, His Sidekick, and the Cornbread Incident	99
35	Cigarettes in the Teepee	101
36	The Little Dirt Basketball Court	104
37	Booger Red	107
38	The Time We Took Mama to Rasslin'	110
39	Up (to My Waist in) the Creek	113

40	Running from a Whoopin'	116
41	His Versus Hers	118
42	I Only Cheated Once	120
43	Lessons From Pop	123
44	Abercrombie Jumps on the Grill	126
45	Don't Ever Say You've Never	129
46	Status Symbol of Choice	133
47	A Near Tragedy	136
48	Building a Baseball Program from the Ground Up	140
49	Worst to First on the Cool Chart	148
50	Exception to the Brother Code	151
51	Prom and My Parents' Peculiar Habit	153
52	Doug Flutie and a Load of Firewood	156
53	Remembering Mike	159
	Conclusion	163
	Bonus Chapter: You Thought Like Parker's Dog	169

ACKNOWLEDGMENTS

To Jesus Christ, who called me in 1985 and has led me to and through some unexpected leaps of faith since then. Ultimately, my story is His story.

To my wife, Loretta, who has walked with me through the craziness for almost 22 years now. I love building our family's legacy with you.

To my kids—Ashton, Garrett, and Drew. Remember when you used to ask "Grampy" to tell you a story? Well, here's 53 of them (plus a bonus chapter) for you to hold on to for a lifetime. Never forget to tell...and re-tell the stories.

To every member of my family, no matter which generation or how you came into the family. You're family. Your contributions to this project, no matter how great or small you may have considered them, are priceless. These are our stories and our values, now shared with the world.

To my friend Scott. You have been such a champion on my behalf as I took a leap of faith to step into a brand new career as a writer and speaker. Never underestimate the power of encouragement and accountability with integrity.

To two teachers, Ann Knight and Leigh Ann Scharr, who believed in my writing ability long before this project was even a dream. Thank you for challenging me across the decades.

To my team of volunteer editors: Kevin, our conversations about the book while we were in Haiti gave me a new energy to make the book better. Lou, I can't tell you how much it meant to me that even when I was no longer your boss, you still wanted to invest in me and my book. Tracy, you saw through to some of the deeper aspects of my stories and helped me communicate them better. And to all the members of my family who read the manuscript, I knew all along that you would be by toughest audience. Thank you for being gentle but honest in your criticism.

To each person who backed this project financially, thank you from the bottom of my heart. I must say, your generosity was the most humbling part of preparing this book for publication.

To my church family at Colonial Hills Church, thank you for believing in me as "just me."

To everyone who picks up this book to read it. Thank you for taking a chance on a brand-new writer and for taking the time to read this book. My hope is that you will pass along positive values where you work, where you go to school, where you play, and—most importantly—in the place where you call home.

FOREWORD

Of all the things that went on at family reunions at my Grandma's house when I was a boy—the meals, the caravan to the graveyard, sleeping on a feather mattress—of all of that, my favorite part was when everybody gathered in the living room after supper and told stories. Now, this wasn't an organized event. No one announced, "All right, it's story time!" It just sort of happened. It was the logical thing to do when a bunch of folks got together and sat down, for them to tell stories about (or tell stories *on*) each other.

In later years I have come to the conclusion that those stories are a great part of what makes up my family's DNA. We are connected to our roots through those stories. We discovered we were a part of something way larger than just ourselves from hearing about Granddaddy's adventures in the Smokey Mountains when he and Grandma were first starting out...and the fish that got away that grew bigger with each telling. We discovered not only what happened but also people's reactions to what happened. We learned some life lessons.

I immediately gleaned from Al Ainsworth's collection of tales and recollections he has put together in his *Lines In The Gravel* book that, obviously his is a story-family, too. And his stories are more than just entertainment. Some of them are funny. Some are serious. Some bring a sad smile. But all of them carry a deeper meaning that applies to more than the situation at hand. They apply to life in general. And what better way to learn about life than from stories from a family who lived it right.

Life's lessons are best taught and best remembered when coupled with stories. Blanch Terry, long-time manager of the Old Courthouse Museum in Vicksburg, told me her father was a history teacher. And she said he always told a story along with his lessons. She told me a few of his tales. I still remember them.

Jesus had quite a bit to say about the best way to live life. And he didn't give us a list of rules to memorize so much as he just couched pretty much everything he wanted to teach in a story.

Al Ainsworth has captured precious capsules of life in his stories, and I come away from them having felt some of the obvious love that underlies them rub off on me. They make me feel as if maybe I had just lived a page in the life of his family. And I like that.

It is too bad we don't have the time or the opportunity to have different generations of the family sit down together today and tell stories like these the way we used to. It would help the younger ones catch on to the love and humor and honor that helped shape the family into what it is. It would help them catch on to who they are and to realize they are a part of something bigger than themselves. And remind them that they ARE a part of it. A part of something that has been going on a long time and has survived by the things learned in these stories. Telling the family stories would move them to laugh, to cry and to pitch in and help someone else. It would move them to then pass values like this on to their children, just like they passed on the DNA that molded their children's physical bodies.

Take a lesson from *Lines in the Gravel* and pass on your family stories that mold spirits and bind people together.

Walt Grayson
Broadcaster/Writer
Host of *Look Around Mississippi* and *Mississippi Roads*

INTRODUCTION

I can relate almost anything in life to *The Andy Griffith Show*. I have been hooked on the show for most of my adult life. I can't tell you the number of times I have responded to a statement or a story with, "That reminds me of an episode of *The Andy Griffith Show*...."

In considering why I wanted to write *Lines in the Gravel (and 52 Other Re-Told Childhood Tales)*, I remembered Ed Sawyer. He was the main character in the "Stranger in Town" episode of *The Andy Griffith Show*. He arrived by bus in Mayberry, unknown to anyone in town. However, he knew intimate details about everyone and called them by name as if he had known them his entire life; he even knew that the ever-awake telephone operator, Sarah, liked to take a pinch of snuff once in a while. One lady thought Ed was from the supernatural world. Barney was convinced that he was a foreign spy, perhaps sent to steal their recipe for marmalade jam or gooseberry pie, and was ready to run Ed Sawyer out of town.

Ed was ready to buy George Sepley's gas station (not Wally's Fillin' Station, the only gas station ever mentioned on any other episode), but his familiarity with the townsfolk scared ol' George out of selling to him. Lucy Matthews, the girl Ed was in love with before ever actually meeting her, was also (rightfully) spooked by him.

Eventually, Andy discovered that Ed had grown up moving all around the country, not really having any roots. His buddy in the Army was from Mayberry, and Ed loved hearing about the town and its people; he even began to subscribe to the town's paper. He so longed for a hometown that he decided to make Mayberry "his hometown." He even began to believe that he *was* from Mayberry and was now making the move to "his hometown." In the end the townspeople warmly received Ed as one of their own (though in typical *Andy Griffith Show* style, he never appeared in another episode.)

What about you? Do you identify more with Ed Sawyer or with one of the locals from Mayberry? As you recall your own childhood, is there a hometown, a home place that comes to mind? Or were you, like Ed, a wanderer with no real place to call home?

I remember as a kid riding with my parents through downtown Jackson, Mississippi, where my parents would point out where their first home used to be; it was a dry cleaners by then. The four of us kids used to joke about Mom and Dad living in a dry cleaner's.

My parents moved into a new home in Star, Mississippi, when I was born in 1966. All these years later, they still live there. The carport is now a den, other rooms have been added, and quite a few outbuildings have been built, but they are still there. (Dad once suggested throwing a roof over the whole 28 acres and being done with it.) So when people ask me where I'm from, I tell them I'm from Star, Mississippi. Sure, I've lived in other places all over the great state of Mississippi since then, but I'm from only one place: Star, Mississippi.

Being able to go back to your childhood home brings a certain stability to life, one that I know not everyone enjoys. Not even most people, I have discovered. I have lived in more than a dozen places since I left home, but I can still go back to where I came from. And I do.

And then there's Kris. I thought about him recently. I have actually thought about Kris often through the years, though I never got to know him well. He was a smallish ninth grade dynamo in an English class I taught about 20 years ago. He couldn't sit still or stay on task or keep his mouth closed for more than a few minutes at a time.

On the first day of school, after getting the particulars of class requirements and expectations out of the way, I would give my students a chance to ask me a few personal questions. I knew that I would get these questions later in an attempt to interrupt the educational process, so on this first day, I attempted to "nip that in the bud." The typical questions were predictable: Are you married? Do you have kids? Where are you from? (Followed by: Did you know Faith Hill?) Where did you go to college? How old are you? Questions like that.

Kris raised his hand as soon as I gave his class the opportunity for questions. He was sitting right in front of my desk, and I could already tell he was the type of student who simply would not be ignored, so I called on him first. His question: "Coach, did yo' Daddy ever whoop you with a 'stansion cord?"

That question continues to haunt me all these years later. I know enough now to know that Kris wasn't just a hyperactive kid trying to get attention with a shocking question (though he certainly accomplished that). I wonder what it was in Kris's life that had precipitated that question. I wonder why Kris had walked in my classroom and voluntarily sat right in front of my desk. Actually, I'm pretty sure that he was seeking attention and affirmation that I must confess that I fell short in giving him.

I wonder if I could have made a difference in Kris's life had I not been so naïve about the different backgrounds from which my students came. I wonder where Kris is now and what he's doing. I wonder how roots, stability, and a place to call "home" would have changed Kris's life. I am left to wonder because I never dug deeper into his life back then, and I have never seen him since the end of that school year. In the strangest sort of way, remembering Kris reminds me of an episode of *The Andy Griffith Show* . . . . I hope that Kris found "his hometown."

My sheltered small town life has intersected with many very different lives since Kris's curious question. Thirteen years as a teacher and coach and eight more as a small groups pastor have opened my eyes to the places from which others have come—and not just their geographical locations. I have heard the circumstances and situations of others and stepped into their lives to get to know them and understand them and even—feebly at times—to try to help them.

I have learned that I do have something to offer people who come from different backgrounds and circumstances than I do. I can offer **normal**. Normal is difficult to define and is even more elusive. Nobody's life is normal, really, but my sisters and brother and I have come to understand that our childhood was about as close to it as we have seen. Further, I would go past *normal* to describe our home as healthy. And that lays on us a burden of responsibility.

When I share my family's stories with others whose homes were nothing like the one of my childhood—and neither are their current homes in most instances—many of them have no hopes of familial health. Others, though, do see a glimmer of hope. They see that while creating a healthy family environment is not easy, that it is possible. Someone has achieved it; someone has been there. For those of us who have achieved some measure of health in our families, we have the responsibility to tell our stories to bring hope to others.

I tell the Ainsworth family story in this book not simply to preserve our favorite stories and not to present our family as any sort of ideal but to attempt to preserve the values that those stories reflect. I call this "values storying." My hope for this book is to begin to create a blueprint by which families (and by extension, churches, schools, teams, businesses, and other organizations) can

4

perpetuate their values by the stories they tell...and re-tell.

So sit back and enjoy *Lines in the Gravel (and 52 Other Re-Told Childhood Tales)*, the stories of our clan that we often tell when we gather as a family. In the back of your mind, though, make mental (and perhaps physical) notes of the stories that you should be preserving and/or creating. Let's preserve our stories and our values by telling the right stories often. Who knows, maybe our version of *normal* will not only strengthen our own families but it may also rub off on a kid like Kris and give him a sense of "hometown."

1 MEET THE FAMILY

With all the various tales to be told in this book, this chapter was the most difficult to write. Oh, it's not that my family is so large that I have forgotten their names or that I have been distant from them. No, the problematic issue is all the nicknames. You can't even begin to know my family without a list of at least some of the nicknames. My dad gave every member of our family multiple monikers and has done the same for the in-laws and the grandkids. The lone exception is my wife, Loretta. With almost 25 years of opportunity now, Dad has yet to find a nickname that would stick to her.

My mom's side of the family is easy. She is an only child. Her parents were Tomp and Mama Tomp. They lived a couple of hours away in North Carrollton, and we only saw them a few times a year. Mom's side of the family was actually quite large, as both Tomp and Mama Tomp came from sizable families. Mom had two sets of double first cousins (brothers marrying sisters—no, not *their own* sisters—I know what you out-of-staters are thinking). She had an Aunt Heber, too, but she couldn't say Heber as a young girl, so she called her Aunt Bubba. So I had an "Aint Bubba." Aside from a couple of family reunions near Kilmichael (out from Winona) and a couple of trips to north Georgia, though, we didn't get to know Mom's side of the family very well.

Dad's side of the family lived nearer, and we interacted with them just about every day. We called Dad's parents Pop and Granny, and they lived on the first house on the left on our road. Uncle Cecil and Aunt Sissy, my dad's younger sister, and their son Sonny lived between Pop and Granny's house and ours. Dad's twin brother, Monroe, and my Aunt Evelyn and their kids Beth, Susan, and Thom lived in Pelahatchie (45 minutes away) and then in Collins (about an hour away), and we just saw them a few times a year.

The nicknames must have started with my dad and my uncle. We never called my uncle *Monroe*, his given name; he has always been Uncle Hob, a shortened form of Hob Nob, to us. No matter where the nickname game started, the introductions get more complex once we focus on the succeeding generations. Meet the family, nicknames and all:

Al (That's me.) – Al Snortavan, Linus, Mr. Flicky.

Lu Ann (my sister, one year younger than me) – Foofer, Foofer Doofer, Ludy Moosy.

Wilagene (my sister, one year younger than Lu Ann) – Spider Spitter Spunter, Spide, Runt, Little Feller.

Andy (my brother, one year younger than Wilagene) – Hankus Pankus Inkus Ikus Unkus Brown (must be said really fast), Lionel, Do' Lionel, Pedrew.

Got all those nicknames? Wait, there are many more:

I married Loretta (again, the anomaly with no nickname), and we have three children: Ashton (Fum Dumplin'), Garrett (Pot Licker), and Drew (Fiz Dobbler, Lil' Pedrew).

Lu Ann married Charlie (Charlie Marker, the Marker). Andy calls them "the Marker and the Moose." Their boys are Ryne (Possum Contattus) and Hayden (Buster).

Wilagene married Stan, who had long hair when they started dating; therefore, Dad tagged him with *Shagnasty*. They have two children, Daniel (Bo Monkey) and Alison (Sookie Fum).

Our family could do an undercover operation of some sort, I'm sure. We have the code names to swing it. Lest you consider yourself overwhelmed and are tempted to give up on the rest of the book, don't worry. Remembering the nicknames is not a prerequisite to your enjoying the remainder of the book; however, you needed this glimpse to appreciate the sophistication of the Ainsworth clan.

I won't give you any more to chew on at this point (say, for instance, our animals and their nicknames). Just enter into our craziness. Though you may shake your head at our silliness, you will find a family that loves telling stories, that loves recalling good (and sometimes not so good) memories, that loves passing along the values of generations past, and that just plain loves one another in our own unique way.

2 THAT DARNED OL' HAPPY MAN AND HIS SAMUNCRIUM

Dad was always carrying on some kind of *samuncrium*. There is so much behind that statement that is difficult to describe, but I'll do my best. Sometimes, there are words that do not translate into English. My friend Dusty, a lifelong missionary, will sometimes insert a Spanish or Portuguese word into an otherwise English sentence because that word more fully expresses what he intends to convey. *Samuncrium* is one of those types of words.

Samuncrium is an example of an "Abboism," a peculiar set of words and phrases that are mostly unique to my family. Some are formerly common sayings from back in the day, but my dad or his dad invented most of them. Dad's nickname from childhood is Abbo, so I have dubbed the lexicon *Abboisms* for posterity's sake. Dad argues that they should be called *Popisms* since my grandfather coined many of the terms, but I'm writing the book, so *Abboisms* they forever shall be.

Samuncrium may be defined in three different contexts: (1) an aphorism used to express disbelief (Any of my siblings: "Dad, Al said he gets the last piece of cake because he is the oldest and smartest." Dad: "Aw, *samuncrium*."), (2) a lighthearted but slightly aggravating frivolity ("You're always carrying on a bunch of *samuncrium*"), and (3) an instance of said frivolity going too far so as to instigate familial antagonism ("All right, you young 'uns, cut out all that confounded *samuncrium!*").

In Dad's case the second context was where he could most often be found in relation to the word: Dad was always carrying on some kind of *samuncrium*. His incessant whistling was a constant, from tunes from his childhood or those invented along the way. (Oh, how I wish I could take you inside my mind as I am writing this so that you could read with the same soundtrack with which I write....) If he wasn't whistling, he was singing. Seemingly every word reminded him of a song, some of which you would recognize and some which you wouldn't. "Do Your Ears Hang Low" comes to mind as one of his favorites.

If Dad wasn't whistling or singing, he was carrying on some kind of *samuncrium* with his collection of Abboisms, adding to them as life events inspired. In moments of uncertainty, for example, he would deepen his voice and ask, "What's I'm 'on do?" (Translated: "What am I going to do?") That one came from Ol' Big Jim, one of Dad's co-workers. Dad's *samuncrium* only seemed to be fueled by a day at work; I guess he spent all day with an assortment of co-workers always up to some sort of shenanigans. And so on and on it went, day after day, always some kind of *samuncrium*.

Mom could have easily become irritated with Dad and all his *samuncrium*. After all, she worked hard all day keeping up with us four children, doing all the tasks of motherhood that would need repeating the following day...and the day after that...and the day after that.... After she returned to the workforce when I was in sixth grade—only to come home to helping with homework, cooking supper, cleaning the kitchen, settling disputes, and so forth—she probably had little energy left to put up with Dad's antics. Mom, however, chose a different path, the path of amusement. She took to calling my dad "that darned ol' happy man."

When Dad was up to some kind of samuncrium, Mom would

feign exasperation. A slight smile. An almost indiscernible shake of her head. And a hint of fondness and love as she would say, "There goes that darned ol' happy man." I suppose she knew that there are a lot worse stations in life than to tolerate a man who liked to express his perpetual state of happiness. Perhaps the harmony of their relationship in that regard is why now, as the leader of my own family, I am always carrying on some kind of samuncrium. I'd like to think that it's because I have become a "darned ol' happy man."

3 WE'RE A COMPETITIVE LOT

We Ainsworths, we're a competitive lot. Perhaps that's because my siblings and I are so close in age. Or maybe because there were six of us competing for less-than-enough leftovers to go around at the supper table. Lu Ann—a feisty enough competitor in her own right—didn't help matters any by marrying Charlie into the family. Wilagene's husband, Stan, smoothes the edges a little bit by laughing at our competitive spirits that are still as strong as ever and quite evident in the next generation of our family. (Stan is also an only child. Hmmm...)

Mom and Dad took advantage of our drivenness during the summers when harvest time came for the peas and butter beans. Dad picked the peas and butter beans most of the time, and Mom waited for us to shell them so that she could clean them, blanch them, and bag them for the freezer. Lu Ann, Wilagene, Andy, and I were the middlemen. Mom and Dad offered us competitive bonuses based on the total weight of beans shelled, bonuses that greatly increased production. (And by bonuses, think the kind that jingles, not the kind that folds.) There's no telling how much extra sleep Mom enjoyed on those summer nights because she knew how to harness the natures of her children for good and not evil.

The four of us, along with our often-cutthroat competitiveness, have an innate sense of fairness. Mom, the official operator of the kitchen scales, could not simply weigh the peas and dole out our bonuses. Oh, no, she had to weigh one kid's bowl, empty that bowl, and weigh every kid's peas in that same bowl. Then, and only then, could there be equal comparison and fair compensation.

Mom had a similar incentive plan for report cards. No matter whether the grade was a six weeks grade, exam grade, semester grade, or yearly grade, each grade on the report card earned the following bonuses: a nickel for an *A*, three cents for a *B*, and a penny for a *C*. Grades of *D* and *F* earned rewards, too, but of a much different type. The money was paid out on the last day of school and never amounted to more than a few dollars. The money was nice, but that wasn't the most important aspect of Mom's incentive plan. Have you ever watched players (and parents and grandparents) in those ridiculous sports leagues where they don't keep score but you can tell some individuals are keeping score anyway? Yeah, it was like that with my sisters and brother with our grades throughout the year. In the end the money we received for good grades was nothing more than our scoreboard.

The competitive fire that I grew up with has served me well most of my life, but there have been exceptions. Like the time when I was racing my cousin John Earl on motorcycles down a gravel road. As the finish line (and the 90-degree turn in the road just on the other side of it) approached, the race was still too close to call. John Earl let off the throttle, and I did not. I won the race, though John Earl rode upright around Dead Man's Curve, and I did not.

The characteristic Ainsworth sense of fairness has also served me well with rare exception. I did choose to stop playing board games with Charlie and Lu Ann for a while for the cause of familial peace. Charlie and I couldn't agree on a common set of rules for Scrabble, and he and Lu Ann had a tendency to "help each other" a little too much for my taste in team games.

She would say something like, "Sweetie, I don't know the answer to this one..."

He would answer something like, "Well, Angel, (insert not-at-all-subtle hint)...."

Their "helping" was a little too sappy for my taste. Understand, though, that Lu Ann and Charlie met in high school, and he kept her supplied with fresh flowers for the first year or so that they dated. And they're still just as happy and sappy as they ever were some 25+ years and a couple of sons later. And I love that about them; I really do...as long as we're not playing board games together.

Now that most of our next generation of kids are entering young adulthood, the Ainsworth family get-togethers are one competition after the other. At our gathering last Christmas, you might have found us playing card games, dice games, guessing games, and unwrap-the-present-with-gloves-on games. All with a winner. You might have found us playing tournaments on the ping pong table in our front entryway, tournaments that Charlie had entered into the tournament app downloaded to his iPad so that byes and choices of table sides would be determined at random by a computer rather than by the Ainsworth clan. (That would have taken a while....) I would give you more interesting details about how the ping-pong tournament played out, but I didn't win, so it doesn't really matter anyway.

4 WILAGENE: BLESS HER HEART

I love both of my sisters, but I sure am glad I was born a male. Oh, I'm not (overly) chauvinistic—it's just that I'm a fan of somewhat normal names. And for my parents, naming boys was an easy task. I go by Al, but my full name is Allen Wade, my grandfathers' middle names. My brother's name is David Andrew (Andy), as mainstream a name as you'll find. My cousin Beth recently researched our family history back to the 1600's, and one of the surprising aspects of the Ainsworth family line was the normality of the names through the centuries.

That long-held tradition ended in our generation with my sisters. My sisters were given more, er, unique names. *Lu Ann* is not too uncommon, at least in the South. The *Lu* is a shortened form of Dad's first name (Luther), and the *Ann* is a shortened form of Mom's name (Annette, with more emphasis on the *Ann* than the *–ette*). And then there's Wilagene....

Wilagene is a peculiar amalgamation of my grandmothers' names. Wilma Thompson (Mama Tomp) was my mother's mother; Mom and Dad just dropped the "m" from her name. Genie Ainsworth (Granny) was my dad's mother; Mom and Dad dropped the "i" from her name, thus arriving at *Wilagene*. (As I write this paragraph, I am anticipating your pause at this moment to "bless her heart.") But wait, it gets worse.

Wilagene is not my sister's first name; that would be Frances, after my Aunt Sissy (Frances Ann). On the first day of school each year, as each teacher would call roll without yet knowing the students, she would inevitably call out, "Frances Ainsworth." To which my sister would have to reply, "It's Wilagene." Bless her heart.

Since we grew up in Star, Mississippi, Wilagene's name was often not articulated very well, even in our family. It often came out more like "Woolagene." That wasn't such a big deal when most everyone said it like that, but my sister has lived away from Mississippi for over 20 years now, and people where she lives tend to enunciate a little more. Imagine family members visiting and calling her "Woolagene" in front of her enunciating friends and neighbors. I can imagine them thinking, "*Where* are you *from*? Bless your heart."

As kids—and, I have to admit, even as adults—we had fun with all the misspellings of Wilagene's name. *Willa Jean* was the most common, and she was tabbed *Wilmagene* on several occasions. *Wilagreen* was one of our favorites. The biggest head-scratcher was the prescription bottle for *Wildazene*. What?!? When she married Stan, my sister's name became Wilagene McElhenney. Bless her heart. I always tell her that it's a good thing she is not famous; autographs would be a bear.

Wilagene never found much camaraderie when it came to her name. When we would stop at a Stuckey's on one of our rare family trips, we would inevitably wind up looking through the coffee cups and key chains with names on them. She knew better than to even get her hopes up. To the best of my knowledge, the only other Willa Jean (close enough when your name is Wilagene) that she ever came across was a bit character in the Ramona and Beezus books by Beverly Cleary. (Even as I type this chapter on my computer, I am distracted by all the red lines under every unrecognized Wilagene.) Bless her heart.

Wilagene has done quite well for herself through the years in spite of her albatross of a name. She was her class valedictorian and has gone on to have several successful careers. When she decides she wants to do something else, jobs find her at twice the salary of her previous job—okay, I exaggerate...a little. She continues to answer the all-too-familiar questions about her name with her same familiar smile, roll of the eyes, and good humor; she carries her name well.

But one question still remains these many years later: though my parents are otherwise intelligent and resourceful people, what were they thinking?!? Bless their hearts.

5 STAR PROPER

Star, Mississippi, is a small dot on the map 18 miles south of Jackson right along Highway 49. Since Star was then and still remains an unincorporated town, its boundaries are nebulous. When I think of the Star of my childhood, I remember what my dad and I now call "Star proper." As kids, my sisters and brother and I could have walked, ridden our bikes, and (eventually) ridden my motorcycle to any place within those boundaries.

Just a tenth of a mile west off the highway was the main inter section of Star. To turn left was to go toward Star Baptist Church. To turn right was to go toward Wesleyanna United Methodist Church. To continue on straight was to go toward the Star Volunteer Fire Department and Rankin Academy. And right there at the intersection was the hub of industry in Star: Mangum's Store. The post office was located inside the store until the Star post office opened in its very own building halfway between the store and the Methodist church in the 1970's.

When my family spends time re-telling the stories of our childhood, I notice an interesting word coming up time and time again: *the*. *The* is a most-often unobserved article used to point out a specific noun as opposed to a general noun (*the* store versus *a* store). While it may also indicate a lack of choice, *the* has endeared itself to me as an article of stability straight from Smalltown, USA.

Allow me to re-describe Star, starting from our house about a mile from the intersection that unofficially marked Star proper:

- From our driveway we would turn right onto *the* road.
- We would follow *the* road around a turn and Aunt Sissy and Uncle Cecil's house, down the hill by Pop and Granny's house, and around a slight turn until *the* road dead-ended into *the* big road, where we would take a right toward town.
- As we neared town, we would cross over *the* railroad tracks and pass *the* fire department.
- Just over the hill from *the* fire department was *the* store. From there we could easily get to *the* Baptist church, *the* Methodist church, *the* post office, or continue on to *the* highway.

Directions were easy. We didn't have to define which fire station, which store, which Baptist or Methodist church. Throughout this book I will be relating different childhood adventures from Star. Occasionally, I will mention *the* this or *the* that. Don't spend your time fretting about which one; chances are, there was just one.

Through the years, as I have told people from different parts of the state and country that I am from Star, Mississippi, I have often been asked something like, "Is that one of those one-traffic-light type of towns?" I would respond, "No, but we're hoping..."

Today, compared to the town of my childhood, Star is booming. It has a birdhouse manufacturer that sends top-of-the-line birdhouses all over the nation. It has a chemical industry and *two* gas stations. It has a Family Dollar Store, known locally as the Star Wal-Mart. It has a Woman's Club, an annual Christmas parade, and an annual 5K run—fittingly, just one of each.

Oh, and Star now has *the* traffic light out where *the* big road crosses *the* highway.

6 A BLACK WELCOME MAT AND MY INHERITANCE

My dad and I have a running joke about my future inheritance. Every time he tells me about a new trip that he and Mom are planning, he always says the same thing: "We're just spending some more of your inheritance."

I always respond the same way: "Go ahead. Spend it how you want. It's not mine to spend, anyway."

I have seen families rip themselves apart over money and things that they won't get to keep long anyway. I have a few items that belonged to my grandparents, long since deceased. Want to know the most valuable item I have that belonged them? A black rubber "Welcome" mat—just a plain, cheap mat that had its place for many years in front of the threshold of the door to Pop and Granny's house. The welcome mat has no value except this: It reminds me of daily conversations with my grandparents on their front porch.

Pop and Granny lived two houses away, just over the hill. My sisters and brother and I would walk to their house to visit every day. The front porch was where most of the conversations took place. It was a simple, concrete porch. The raised middle section of the porch—about ten or twelve feet wide and about four feet deep—hosted two chairs, one on either side of the front door and the aforementioned welcome mat. A step down to either side and areas of similar size to the middle section offered more seating. Pop and Granny had their sides of the porch, and I usually sat in the middle.

That front porch was where Granny quizzed us about our days and told us about hers. It was where Pop would recount comings and goings of the olden days. He would grow increasingly frustrated when I had never heard of Ol' Man So-and-So or where the old So-and-So place was; nonetheless, he would go on to complete his stories. I wish now that I had paid more attention to his unfolding of the affairs of days gone by.

Because the porch itself was cool concrete in hot, humid central Mississippi, it would sweat under the welcome mat. I don't recall when or why I started flipping the mat, but I made it a habit upon my arrival each day. Pop and Granny and I would visit for a spell while the porch dried, and I would flip the mat back over when it was time to go home. I am willing to admit that the habit was perhaps a little OCD, but it became a ritual that I still remember. The mat is outside between my garage doors now, and I still flip it from time to time, giving thanks each time for the pleasant memories that are a much greater inheritance than any worldly possessions they could have left me.

One day, I stand to inherit some of the land that Pop and Granny left to my dad. That's a little presumptuous, I know, because like all the rest of their possessions, it's theirs to do with what they please. No matter what my parents do or do not leave me as an inheritance, they have blessed me beyond measure with a legacy of passed-on wisdom and experiences. They have passed on a legacy that I am reminded of every time I pass by what's left (thanks to my dog Molly) of the simple black welcome mat and give it a good flip.

7 FAMILY NAMES, SOUTHERN NAMES

In Star, Mississippi, keeping up with names took more than a little work. I'm going to take you on a little tour of some of Star's distinctive names and test your ability to keep track of who is who.

Though we are hardly unique, our family is growing its own impressive legacy among firstborn sons. My son Garrett is a fourth-generation Allen. No juniors. His name is Garrett Allen. Mine is Allen Wade. Dad's is Luther Allen. Pop's was Thomas Allen. I don't know at what point this became intentional in our family, but Garrett assures me he plans to continue the unbroken line of *Allens* (with no juniors).

My dad introduces himself to my friends as *the* Allen Ainsworth. I suppose there's truth in that statement. Garrett goes by Garrett, and I go by Al (except for a brief time in elementary school when I was too painfully shy to ask the teacher to call me by my nickname). Pop went by Tom A. Where we are from, that is pronounced as one word, like *Tommay*. That's a pretty common practice because my Aunt Sissy's full name was *Fransann* (Frances Ann), and my dad's first cousin is *Dempsearl* (Dempsey Earl).

Dempsey Earl's oldest son is John Earl, and they lived across the road from Uncle Pete and his son Repete. Actually, his name was James but everybody called him Repete. I was asking my dad one time how we were kin to Uncle Pete, and he told me that we were only distantly related. Dad said there were three brothers, whom he grew up calling Uncle Pete, Mr. Dan, and Cud'n Milton. Speaking of Milton, there was a man who lived down at the other end of our road named Milton Brown. I don't think I ever heard anyone ever call him *Milton*; it was always *Milton Brown*.

There were certainly other unique names. My friend Danny's dad goes by *Tuffy*. (I remember the time he was particularly careful to protect his bald head while on a float trip down the Homochitto River—only to burn the bottom of his feet.) Tuffy's wife goes by *BaBa* (*Bay-Bay*). A kid a few years behind me in school went by *PeeWee*. (He had the distinction of being the only seven-year letterman in baseball of which I am aware. He didn't play in sixth grade, so I'm pretty sure there was a rules infraction that came into play at some point. Shhh – don't tell.)

Still keeping up? I had an Aint Boodie (real name: Annie Ruth) on my dad's side and an Aint Bubba (real name: Heber) on my mom's side. If you don't know what an *aint* is, then you ain't from the South. I'm here to help even my northern friends through this tour, though—an *aint* is an aunt.

I've saved the best for last: my Uncle Hob. That's short for Hob Nob. Don't think that's his real name? I have seen it on his ID (understanding that where I'm from, the back of one's belt is recognized as a valid form of identification). Uncle Hob and my dad are twin brothers, known collectively as *Abbo* and *Nungo*. Actually, Uncle Hob's real name is Monroe (with more *Mon-* than *-roe*), but most people I know just call him Hob Nob.

Now, you might get the picture that people from Star are just a bunch of hicks with backward naming practices. If that's the case, let me ask you a question: Whose head is spinning right now trying to keep up with all the names? Those of us from Star – we got this.

8 THE STORE (OR THE DE-FLAGPOLING OF EDWARD BONE)

The store was located in the heart of Star at the intersection of the streets now called Mangum Drive and Main Street. The tan-bricked, concrete-floored store had a giant yellow border around the edge of the roof with bright red letters proclaiming "Mangum's Store." Back then, the roads at the intersection had no names, and Mangum's Store might as well not have, either. We simply called it "the store."

The store's wide, multi-angled front meant that except for their busiest times, all the customers could park right by the sidewalk that framed the front of the store. There were no lined parking spaces, just room to park. There was a flagpole about 15-20 feet high to the right of the door as you faced the store because the post office at one time was just inside and to the right.

I remember the flagpole because it provided entertainment and adventure for those of us kids who were waiting for a ride to a baseball game as we saw how far up the pole we could scale. It's the same flagpole from which Edward Bone fell one day. Edward was more adept at shinnying up that pole than the rest of us, but he lost his grip that day and down he came in a moment of terror, for himself and for those of us who observed his plummet. Edward survived to climb again, but on that day, he was...wait for it...a broken Bone.

Every Saturday, we Ainsworth kids would get our allowances—$1.00 for the better part of our childhood—all of which would be spent at the store. Sometimes, Mom or Dad drove us there, sometimes we rode our bikes, and sometimes we walked. (Though the store was only a mile from our home, we were in the habit of conserving energy if we possibly could.) There were occasions when circumstances caused us to miss our usual Saturday journey to the store, but we would always find a day during the following week to get us back on schedule. On these days, Lu Ann and Wilagene would start walking toward the store, timing their walk so that Dad would see them on his way home from work, pick them up and turn around and take them to the store. The energy they saved from that tactic has likely added years onto their lives.

The store had groceries and dog food and other such necessities toward the back of the building, but we kids rarely made it past the first 20 feet or so, where all the candy, chips, and other snacks were located. We each knew just what we would buy; rest assured, there would *not* be any change coming back with us. My usual purchases were a Coke (and we Southerners know that "Coke" means any carbonated beverage), a bag of chips, some Now 'n Laters or a moon pie or a Push Up (orange sherbet on a stick), and maybe some bubble gum. Yes, a dollar went a lot further in those days. Plus, the kind ladies* who worked the register never charged us kids tax on our purchases. That fact never ceases to be remembered and appreciated as we recount the days of going to the store.
*I avoid the use of the names of the kind ladies in case there are pending Mississippi State Tax Commission investigations into under-reporting of sales taxes from the 1970's. Far be it from me to cause these ladies to spend their prime years locked up. You never know, these days.

When I was in junior high, Slush Puppies in a helmet were a reason to visit the store every day. These were the miniature Major League Baseball helmets that are still popular today, but they were the next big thing then. The store would only have a few teams' helmets at a time, and I was intent on collecting them all to place on the cardboard standings board that the makers of the Slush Puppy had so conveniently made available to collectors like myself. By that time in my childhood, I had a little motorcycle, so I rode out to the store every day to see if a new helmet that I did not yet have had become available. I had begun to mow our yard and a couple of others by then, so I had disposable income to spend on Slush Puppies—every day, if necessary. When several helmets that I didn't have became available at the same time, my sisters and brother received complimentary Slush Puppies so that I could be assured not to miss a single helmet. Eventually, I collected them all; I still have them in my attic somewhere, though it is now an incomplete collection because of the addition of teams to Major League Baseball since my childhood. Oh, well.

Sometime during our growing-up years, the Mangums sold the store, and though it was still called Mangum's Store (as if the name mattered to us anyway), it just wasn't the same. The new owners charged us tax, which I believe was the beginning of their undoing. Of course, the new gas station/convenience store's opening out on the highway didn't help, either. Mangum's Store eventually closed, and the building was torn down a few years after that. Though the location remains desolate now, for the Star of our childhood memories, "the store" will always remain the centerpiece of town.

9 HOW GRANNY CAME TO BE CALLED GRANNY

Granny was the spunkiest of all my grandparents. My father's mother, she was considerably younger than all of my other grandparents, about a decade-and-a-half younger than Pop, and she could certainly relate to her grandchildren. Granny was about five feet tall (and that's generous) and couldn't have possibly weighed in at much more than a hundred pounds, if even that much. She wore glasses and wore her white hair short, sometimes curly and sometimes straight. Think a slightly softer version of Granny from *The Beverly Hillbillies*. And, oh, was our Granny fun!

I remember thinking how cool Granny was to stay up late every New Year's Eve, knowing that we kids would be heading over the hill to her house at a few minutes before midnight to celebrate with her. I'm sure there were plenty of other grandparents who stayed up to ring in the New Year, but Granny was the only one who stayed up with *us*. Every year, my parents would warn us not to wake her up if she had already gone to bed. And every year, Granny didn't disappoint us; she might have already been in bed, but she was always awake and waiting for us.

Granny was also our weekday source of Coca-Cola. We only drank Coke on Friday and Saturday nights at our house; it was Kool-Aid the rest of the week. When the whole family visited Granny and Pop's together, we kids would run ahead and alert

Granny that Mom and Dad were coming. She knew the drill: We would all visit for a few minutes before she would act as if she had just had a novel idea: "Hey, do you kids want to go back and fix yourself a Coke?"

"Sure," we would respond with mock surprise. Then, we would march back toward the kitchen to fix ourselves a Coke just like we did every single day. We had held to our home training of not asking for something to drink, and we were still able to enjoy our Cokes with innocent consciences because Granny had played her usual role as catalyst. She had a similar system worked out with our older cousin, Sonny, and his parents. He would signal "1" for a Coke and "2" for a snack, and Granny would respond accordingly.

My brother and I loved to watch the Saturday baseball Game of the Week with Granny at her house. I think she enjoyed watching us watch the game and get into it like we did more than she actually enjoyed watching the game itself. On the rare occasions that Andy and I would miss the Game of the Week, Granny would tell us that we missed a good game. We would ask her who won, and she usually couldn't remember, "but it was a good game." We would press a little more and ask her who played, and she usually couldn't remember that, either, "but it was a good game." That was our Granny.

My sisters remember Granny and all of the beautiful flowers in her yard. Granny would gladly meet them in the yard with her scissors and cut them bouquets of flowers so that they could practice their wedding marches up her front walkway. That's the essence of our Granny; she was not only willing to sacrifice what was hers for us, but she wanted to join in on the fun, too!

One day, I became curious as to how Granny had come to be known to her grandkids as Granny. So many grandparents today just go by whatever the first grandchild happens to call them. Not so with Granny; her grand-parental moniker was a deliberate selection. She was of the mind that whatever her grandchildren would call her would define much of the rest of her life, so she chose carefully. Her response to my question of her choice went something like this:

"Well, I knew I didn't want to go by *Grandmother* because that's too formal, and I'm just not a very formal person. Most of the other grandmothers were going by *Grandma*, and I didn't want to be like everybody else. And I didn't want to be called *Nanny*, either, 'cause I'm not a goat. So I just decided on plain old *Granny*."

So, Granny she became and Granny she remained. No one would ever accuse her of being formal, and she was certainly unique among grandmothers. To my knowledge, she never exhibited any of the characteristics of a goat with the exception of a little stubborn streak. But she sure made an amazing Granny.

10 AH AND EE (AND THE TRAGIC CONVERTIBLE ACCIDENT THAT TOOK THEIR LIVES)

Ah and Ee had to die when they drove their red convertible into the lake near the big red-and-white-striped beach umbrellas at Plantation Shores. They just had to. After all, I was starting first grade that fall, and you simply don't start school with imaginary friends. So, with great reluctance on the part of both of my younger sisters, we had to part ways with Ah and Ee. I'm not sure why it had to be in such tragic fashion (finality, a threshold crossed, perhaps?); I only know that it had to happen.

Ah and Ee had been such good imaginary friends. I don't remember too much about them now, whether they were boyfriend and girlfriend, or brother and sister—maybe neither. I do remember that they drove a really cool red convertible and took time to be friends with a six-, a five-, and four-year-old. Cool points for us, for sure. Too bad they had to drown in the lake at Plantation Shores over near the red-and-white-striped beach umbrellas.

Another part of Ah and Ee's story that I don't really remember is why we invented them in the first place. My mom had been a lonely only child and wanted to have enough children of her own to keep one another company, so there were (and still are) four of us, each separated by only about a year. So it wasn't like we didn't have anybody with whom to play.

I guess maybe imaginary friends are part of every child's creative process, even if there are plenty of other kids around. Oh, and the fact that we grew up in the pre-Atari era probably had something to do with our active imaginations and our creation of Ah and Ee, too. So, create them we did. Too bad they had to die when I started school. Such a shame that their red convertible was destroyed in the lake, too; it was one fine automobile.

As my family was sitting around a couple of years ago re-telling tales from childhood, one of my sisters dropped a bombshell on me: *Ah and Ee had miraculously survived their purported drowning in the lake at Plantation Shores over near the red-and-white-striped beach umbrellas, and their cool red convertible had been restored.*

I couldn't believe it.

That part of my childhood, so neatly (albeit tragically) cut off and put away, had been resurrected in my sisters' imaginations; after all, they had figured, *I* was the one starting school, not them. Ah and Ee had survived to gradually drive off in their red convertible into Ainsworth childhood lore. I chose to forgive my sisters' subversion. I'm just glad Ah and Ee are okay and hope they are handing out cool points to other little kids with vivid imaginations today.

11 STILL SITTIN' HERE WHEN I GET BACK!

My parents' house today looks like a normal, middle-class home. However, the same house in my childhood was considerably smaller. My parents moved into this house when they brought me home from the hospital. In 1966, the house consisted of a kitchen that doubled as a tiny eating area, a living area (not really a separate room), a small bathroom, and two small bedrooms. Since then, two bedrooms have been added to one end of the house, the carport has been walled in to become a step-down den at the other end, and the former living area is now a dining area.

After the four of us kids moved out, Dad removed a wall between two of the bedrooms to give he and Mom a bigger bedroom. They added a bathroom off of their bedroom and a hot tub (that I have never seen used though Mom assures me that it was used nightly for a long time) on a little deck outside of their bathroom. The bedroom formerly known as Andy's and my room became an office, and an entryway to the never-used front door was added. Finally, they added a sunroom to the back of the house. The house, though now twice the size as the one I was brought home to, is still quite cozy when all of us and our families are there at any one time.

Though the house grew to match our growing family's needs, the four of us children remember crowding around the big console

TV in the original living area. Dad's chair with ottoman sat directly in front of the TV; the best seat for TV viewing was beside him in his chair but, alas, there wasn't room for all of us beside him. To the right of Dad's chair was a long, dark green vinyl couch whose line of sight to the TV stretched from a pretty decent view to practically out of sight.

Jockeying for television viewing position began early each evening for our favorite family shows like *Little House on the Prairie*, *Happy Days*, and *The Waltons*. To procrastinate on one's homework was risking having to strain to get a glimpse of Richie, Ralph, Potsie, and the Fonz's latest adventure from the end of the couch. And none of us wanted that.

Scoring a good seat for that evening's entertainment was no guarantee of keeping it, however. The ringing of the phone—which usually led to all us kids yelling "Telephone!" —had the potential to open up a seat nearer the TV. So did the inevitable call to the bathroom. As was normal with my competitive but fair-minded siblings, and me we found a way to circumvent the "stealing" of seats.

The unwritten rules were simple, though—true to form in my family—not as simple as they could have been. When we would need to leave the room for a moment or two, we announced, "Still sittin' here when I get back!" This agreed-upon declaration had to be heralded before one could leave his or her perch. To declare one's seat reservation *after* leaving its space was allowed *only if* that seat had not yet been swiped. The varying scenes played out something like this:

RRRRRIIIINNNNGGGG!

"Telephone!!!"

"Lu Ann, it's for you."

"Still sittin' here when I get back!"

(phone conversation ends)

"Andy, get out of my seat."

"You got up."

"I said I was still sittin' here when I got back."

(Andy moping back to the end of the couch)

Or it might play out like this:

RRRRRIIIINNNNNGGGG!

"Telephone!!!"

"Al, it's for you."

(I hurry to phone)

(phone conversation ends)

"Wilagene, get out of my seat."

"You got up and didn't call it."

(Argument ensues. Referees intervene.)

(My moping back to the end of the couch)

I have a friend whose family used ghost men to solve this problem in his house. Andy and I used ghost men frequently as imaginary runners in our baseball games. When there are only a few people playing baseball or kick ball, you must employ imaginary players for the game to work. If only I had known then that ghost men were so versatile, I would have never lost a prime seat to one of my siblings. But, alas, I didn't know.

A larger den brought an end to those childhood squabbles. Everyone had about as good a view as anybody else for *The Cosby*

Show, *Family Ties*, and *The Dukes of Hazzard*. When Bo and Luke broke through the road construction sign and soared into the air with a big "Yeee-haww!" (Remember that episode?), we could all see it just fine.

As our extended family has grown over the years, we will sometimes find ourselves watching a show together at one of our houses. Something will call (usually) Wilagene out of the room, and she will turn to us with a slight smile and a glint in her eyes and proclaim, "Still sittin' here when I get back." And we'll tell the story of our little childhood home in Star, Mississippi, to our kids once again.

12 WHEN POP CAME DOWN

Pop didn't come down to our house much. Perhaps it was because we kids visited he and Granny at their house pretty much every day. Perhaps it was because he was into his seventh decade by the time the four of us came along. Whatever the reason, it was a rare occasion and always a treat when Pop hiked the couple of hundred yards over the hill from his house to ours. Usually, a scout would come and alert the rest of the gang, "Pop is coming! Pop is coming!"

In our early childhood years, if Pop was coming, that meant that his dog Wormy was a step behind. Wormy was Pop's faithful sidekick, a roly-poly Manchester whose physique belied his name. When Pop would walk anywhere, Wormy followed about a single step behind with his eyes fixed to the ground. If Pop stopped, Wormy ran into him.

When Pop came down, there were a couple of reasons for excitement for us kids. First, Pop usually had a handful of candy in his pocket. Second—and more impressive to little kids growing up in the country—he often had an apple. Now, I don't remember any of the apples themselves being overly impressive. However, Pop could peel an apple all the way around without breaking the peel. And that was about as worthy of pride in our grandfather as the knowledge that he had once won a blue ribbon in the standing broad jump at the county fair.

Standing behind our house and leaning against the butane tank, Pop would start peeling his apple with his pocketknife. Round and round he would go as little eyes gazed with fascination as the peel hanging from the apple grew longer and longer until, finally, he held it up as another completed masterpiece. I always wanted to eat the peel from Pop's apple because, well, an apple peel that has been kept in one piece is tastier than a peel that has been broken, right?

Over the years Pop came down to our house less and less. Wormy died and was replaced by Honkey. Yes, Honkey. All the other dogs on the hill were black, and this little mutt was white, so Pop named him Honkey (the '70's equivalent of calling a white person *cracker*). Unlike Wormy, he was an equal-opportunity little fella, showing no favoritism between Pop and Granny. Honkey's finest moments came during the old TV show *Emergency*. Every week, as the call came into the station declaring that week's fully engaged structure fire, the fire engines would roll out, lights flashing and sirens blaring. Honkey, sitting underneath a table between Pop's and Granny's chairs, would howl in perfect time and with perfect pitch along with the fire engines. In fact, his pitch was so indiscernible from the television speakers that I later dubbed him "surround sound before there was surround sound."

Pop passed away while I was in college many years ago now. Most of my memories of him are centered on the old house that sat just over the hill from where my parents still live. His and Granny's old house is gone now, too, but the memories remain. And though I have never tried to master the art of peeling the apple at which Pop (and my dad after him) were so adept, I'll never forget that special feeling as a small child when Pop came down.

13 YUCKY WATER AND THE GRUMPS

We didn't eat out at restaurants very much when I was a kid. There was one main reason for this: the nearest restaurant was approximately 16 miles away from Star up Highway 49 in Pearl. There are plenty of restaurants now in Florence and Richland (which was then known as Plain), but other than a couple of hamburger stands like the Chuck Wagon, there was nothing closer in my early childhood. Occasionally, though, the six of us would pile into the white, two-door Gran Torino and eat out as a family at McDonald's, Dog 'n Suds, Pasquale's Pizza, or Bonanza.

I have memories peculiar to each of the restaurants I mentioned. I remember opening the door at McDonald's and hearing "Welcome to McDonald's!" before the door was even completely open. I remember my dad feeding our entire family there for less than $10. Dog 'n Suds was where I discovered frosted mug root beer...mmmm. Pasquale's was where I first ate an entire medium pizza by myself as a young teenager (a rite of passage, if you ask me). And Bonanza was where Andy spilled his root beer on everybody at the kids' table. (He also correctly predicted that he would never live it down.)

Bonanza was also where we kids called an end run around our parents' decision not to buy us dessert. We were sitting at a separate booth—a sort of public kids' table—when this edict came down. Well, the sugar packets were right there on the table for Bonanza's customers, and we were Bonanza's customers, so we took a few packets each and considered them our dessert. Mom and Dad weren't out any more money, desserts were mostly sugar anyway, and we were still within the letter if not the spirit of the law. Sometimes, you just have to improvise.

When we re-tell the stories centered around our infrequent restaurant visits, though, two parts of the trip always come up: the yucky water and the grumps. Before significant work was done a number of years ago at the Highway 49-Interstate 20 interchange, there was an swampy-looking area on the east side of 49 where water collected. It had no outlet and was thus covered most of the time by a slimy green film. One of us called it *yucky* when we were little, so *the yucky water* it became.

The grumps were traffic strips just past the yucky water that warned of the traffic light at the intersection of Highways 49 and 80. When a vehicle passed over these strips, it made a noise something like, "Grrrrruuummmp!" Thus, the name. There were five sets of grumps. This was important because you did NOT want to "be" the grumps. And when you were five years old in my family, you WERE the grumps. It was one of those things that kids argue about that adults can't quite comprehend:

"An-dy's the gru-umps!"

"I am not!"

"Yes you are. You're five years old!"

"I don't care! I am NOT the grumps!"

"Yes you are!"

"KIDS!!!"

Somewhere around the beginning of my high school years, after Plain became Richland, the Dairy Queen opened on the south side of the hill just before the yucky water and the grumps. This became our restaurant of choice. Full Meal Deals were all the rage. They included a coin that you could redeem after your meal for the sundae of your choice. Seems like I also remember some type of scratch-off game that was pretty popular, too. Mainly, though, we liked the Dairy Queen because we began to eat out more often as a family, and that was always a treat. And we didn't have to pass by the yucky water or go over the grumps to get there.

Sometimes, I wonder how other families identified the yucky water and the grumps. Did they even notice them, or were they just part of the landscape? Were any other little kids afraid of going over the bridge on Highway 49 and drowning in the yucky water? Were they ever accused of being the grumps? Am I the only one who ever ponders *samuncrium* like this? I am grateful I have my parents and sisters and brother to join me in this common bond of memory and musing.

14 A MOST UNUSUAL CROP

Late spring always meant Dad's disking the ground just past the barbed wire fence behind our house in preparation for planting the family garden. After a couple of days of preparing the rows and fertilizing the soil, we would all prepare for planting. All of us except Mom and Andy. Mom—well, she would have plenty to do later in the season. And Andy—well, evidently, being the youngest had its privileges.

Planting time was always the favorite part of garden season for my sisters and me. Dad would give us the bag of peas or butter beans or whatever it was that we were planting at that particular time and give us instructions on how many seeds to plant in each hole. Dad usually settled on four: "one for the cutworm, one for the crow, one to die, and one to grow." He would then set out down one of the seemingly endless rows, using a hoe to dig the holes into which we would drop seeds. He would finish a couple of rows and then come back behind us to cover the holes and give them the familiar two-tap tamp. This was a job I would inherit when I got a little older, one that I tried my best to do just like Dad.

Lu Ann, Wilagene, and I would return to the house after a hard day's planting to see what Andy had gotten himself into while we were busy working in the garden. It was, after all, totally unfair to us that he didn't have to work with us just because he was the youngest. More often than not, we would find him in his room with his shirts spread all over his bed. My brother had a fascination with shirts when he was little, and we would hear him saying things like, "Mr. Blue Shirt went to see Mr. Green Shirt and they went over to Mr. Red Shirt's house." We always gave him a hard time about playing with his shirts, but I suppose he had what he thought was the last laugh. After all, he was playing with those shirts while we were doing hot, sweaty work out in the garden. We, however, still have the last laugh today for reasons that you will soon discover.

We kids would get a break from the garden for the next few weeks or so of the growing season until the vines grew across the rows. Then, as Dad ran the rototiller down the middle of the rows, we would hold the vines back so that he could avoid running over them. This was a job we would hurry to because none of us wanted the row on the side of the tiller's exhaust. To get the side with the exhaust meant much stretching and twisting and turning to avoid a mouthful of smoke.

Our next major task would come with the shelling of peas and butter beans. Andy would join us for shelling on the back steps, where we competed for cash prizes. I don't remember Andy ever winning the first prize for most beans shelled, and we usually fussed at him for wasting time and not doing his part in helping us get finished. Eventually, we would complete our part of the work, and Mom would clean, blanch, and bag the peas or beans. I remember eating homegrown peas, butter beans, or string beans at almost every meal (except Friday and Saturday suppers; those were hamburger and hot dog nights, respectively).

Andy's lack of participation in the garden process proved to be his undoing at one point in his childhood. Though I remember Andy spending precious little time in our own garden, he would venture next door to visit with Aunt Sissy and Uncle Cecil while they worked in their garden. As he tells it, he would ask them what they were planting and then proceed to disagree with whatever they told him it was. (He was ornery like that.) On a day when he was about six or seven years old, Aunt Sissy—ever the prankster—told him she was planting chicken and dumplings, and Andy disagreed, as always. He quizzed Mom and Dad about it that night, and they confirmed his doubts that chicken and dumplings could be grown in a garden.

The following day, Aunt Sissy took off work early—she really was serious about her pranking—and bought several cans of chicken and dumplings and "planted" them. When Andy got home from school that day and wandered up to her garden, he found Aunt Sissy with rake in hand. They went through their usual routine: Andy's asking what she was doing that day, Aunt Sissy's responding that she was getting ready to dig up the chicken and dumplings, and Andy's refusing to believe her. With his lack of agricultural experience, Andy also had no idea of the days-to-harvest concept, so as Aunt Sissy began to dig for these chicken and dumplings that she had just "planted" *the day before*, Andy looked on with doubtful curiosity. Then, it happened: Aunt Sissy began to dig up can after can of the most perfect chicken and dumplings that you ever did see!

Andy raced home in amazement. Aunt Sissy had disproved his own doubts and the doubts of even his own parents, and he was holding the proof! I don't think my mom appreciated this little prank very much, picking on her baby and all. My sisters and I still declare that had he spent a little more time actually working in our own garden, perhaps he would not have been so easily duped.

In a family of naïve kids growing up in Smalltown, USA, the tales of the most naïve are the most often re-told. With us, there was always plenty of material. Enough for at least a whole book, as it turns out.

15 ONE THOUSAND LAPS AROUND THE CARPORT

Our tiny living area was soon to become a dining area. Dad and some of his friends were taking in the carport to become our new super-sized den—at least by comparison. That left precious little time for my record-setting performance.

I began that day like I had many Saturdays before it, taking advantage of the empty carport by riding my bike around in circles. I had—and still have—the habit of counting as I am attending to different trivial matters. Counting steps while I walk. Counting cars as I drive. Counting breaths as I try to fall asleep.

As I was riding my bike around the carport on this particular day, I began counting laps. I never intended to make this an all-day venture but as I kept riding and riding and counting and counting, the laps began to mount and my imagination began to soar. I determined to ride 1,000 laps that day. Round and round I went, hour after hour. I took breaks from time to time, but I was persistent in my quest, always remembering to pick up the count where I had left off.

I had told no one of my pursuit of 1,000 laps around the carport. In my mind, though, the Wide World of Sports production crew was certainly on their way to film this momentous occasion, and the crowd was brimming with excitement. However, none of the folks on Ainsworth Road in Star, Mississippi, were even aware of the history in the making right under their noses.

Around the middle of the afternoon, one thousand laps firmly in my grasp, I set out for the culmination of my dazzling feat. The imaginary crowds reached a fever pitch as the 900's clicked by...925, 950, 975. Finally, the one-thousandth lap! But oh no! Trouble on the home stretch! Instead of kicking backward on the pedal for the brakes, I pushed forward and accelerated over the edge of the carport. The imaginary crowd groaned as a terra cotta flowerpot proved no match for my runaway bike that went crashing to the ground, its rider in tow.

Reality quickly replaced my day in Fantasyland as I discovered that the plain clay flowerpot demolished in my fall just so happened to be one of my mom's favorites, if her reaction was any indication. To be fair to her, she had no idea what an epic achievement her eldest had just accomplished. I was just left to pick up the pieces.

And pick up the pieces I did. Mom had kicked up such a ruckus over the flowerpot that Dad pitched in to help me put it back together again. He brought out a roll of the ugliest masking tape I have ever seen, pistachio green with diagonal brown stripes accenting it, just perfect for taping up a favorite shattered flowerpot. Dad and I meticulously taped that flowerpot until it was whole again—the ugliest flowerpot you ever did see, but whole again.

I learned an important lesson that day. When you're coming off the crowning achievement of your life, the adoring crowds can vanish in a heartbeat at the first sign of trouble. Then, you can be grateful to have just one person to help you pick up the pieces of a shattered dream.

16 GOODIES WITH GRANNY

Granny always had goodies for her grandchildren. She started with my cousin Sonny, who is six years older than I am, and carried on with the four of us, who rarely missed a day visiting with her and Pop. Aside from the days when our parents were present—when we collaborated with Granny on an elaborate set of signs to indicate that the time had come for her to present us with an invitation for snacks and Cokes—we were free to go to Granny's kitchen on our own and help ourselves to her goodies. We would typically engage in conversation for a few minutes before giving in to the allure of whatever delectable goodies awaited us in the kitchen.

Granny loved to bake, so Granny's goodies usually consisted of a homemade cake or pie. She convinced me early on that a crumbled cake was a tastier cake. The evidence from her body of work never contested that, so I am still prone to dive right in to a less-than-perfect-looking cake. Granny's apple pies and chocolate pies are still the best I've ever eaten. Her chess squares, replicated incredibly well by my Aunt Sissy, were amazing. I could go on and on....

I graded Granny's goodies on a sliding scale. Cakes and pies were certainly top shelf, and cookies were right up there, too. Sometimes, though, we had to settle for something a little lower on the goodie grade. I remember instant pudding and Jello-O (with fruit cocktail, of course) as occasional substitutes for the best stuff. On rare occasions the snacks were of the store-bought variety, another notch down the scale. Jackson's big, round lemon cookies, slightly stale, are still a favorite of mine.

And then there was the lowest level of Granny's goodies: fruit. On the extremely rare occasions that Granny had not baked anything nor bought anything at the store for our snacks, she would open a can of fruit for our enjoyment. We certainly appreciated her effort but, well, we could have fruit at home. Fruit was good for you. But if that's all Granny had, we didn't want to be rude and refuse it. (And I don't remember ever leaving any fruit cocktail, peaches, pears, or any other fruit in the bowl.)

A level or two back up the goodie scale from any store-bought fruit, though, were "real" peaches that had been frozen from the growing season before. Granny served them half-thawed and covered with sugar. Oh, yeah, that was good stuff. *Those* peaches were better than any other fruit, better than store-bought cookies, and almost on par with some of Granny's baked goodies.

Granny's goodies were a regular, dependable part of our daily routine. That's why one particular day stands out so vividly in my memory. I went to Pop and Granny's to visit one afternoon after school, conversed with them for the requisite five minutes or so, and headed back to the kitchen. I went through the mental goodie checklist upon arriving in the kitchen. Check the kitchen table—no cake or pie. Check the counter—nothing there, either. Check the cabinet—hmm, no store-bought cookies. Check the refrigerator (or the icebox, as Pop still called it)—no Jell-O or pudding or...wait, there in the back! It was a large bowl of peaches, fully thawed, a little pale, and not covered with sugar, but I could at least fix that part. Granny had not let me down.

I raked some peaches into a smaller bowl. I have had a sweet tooth for as far back as I remember, and I anticipated the syrupy goodness of peaches in their own juice, though I had noticed that in addition to the paler color of the peaches, there wasn't as much juice as usual. Someone else must have beaten me to the peach bowl. I couldn't get too upset about that; I had always tipped the bowl and enjoyed the juice myself when I discovered the bowl first. Regardless, I had poured my Coke, and I had my snack ready to take back to the front porch, where Granny and Pop were sitting. As per my habit, I took a quick bite before walking back through the house.

"Ewww!" I exclaimed as I spat the "peaches" back into the bowl. Granny turned the corner into the kitchen right about then and laughed at me eating my snack of...*rutabagas*! A rutabaga is a root vegetable, a type of turnip that in no way tastes like a peach. I know that...now. Granny amusingly apologized for not having any goodies for me that day, but the damage had been done. I don't remember there ever being another day when Granny didn't have some type of snack for us to enjoy, but I vividly remember biting into that piece of rutabaga. I will ***never again in my life*** eat a rutabaga! At least not knowingly

17 LINES IN THE GRAVEL

The bus, Number 58 if my old memory serves me correctly, regularly picked up and dropped off the children of Florence Elementary School who lived in our area. The children in the third house on the left of the then-unnamed road in Star, Mississippi, were right there at the end of their gravel driveway every morning, lined up and ready to board the bus. There were four of us, each separated by one year in age from the next.

To the outside eye, this may have seemed the most normal sight in the world. Just kids waiting on the bus. Just like all the other kids on Bus 58. But the world probably didn't notice the lines in the gravel. . . .

The four of us kids in the Ainsworth house there on what is now—well, Ainsworth Road—argued regularly and profusely about the most important of topics: how to line up for the bus. I am the oldest and felt it was part of my inherent blessing *as* the oldest to be first in all things. My brother, Andy, the youngest, felt cheated by birth order of all things good; the front of the bus line would have simply been logical reparation for this injustice in his life. My sisters in either of those instances were in the middle still; with both girls having been endowed with an innate and acute sense of fairness, any scenario that placed a boy at the front of the bus line was clearly out of bounds. The quarrels over our bus line order became regular and profuse.

The escalating battles over bus line order called for an intervention . . . by Mom. When none of our four action plans was agreeable to any of the others, Mom presented a fifth plan: a rotation. *A rotation?!?* We could have never come with something so simple, yet so ingenious! (We were little kids, after all.) We would each have a day in each place in the line—including the glorious day each week that each of us was first—and we would rotate on Fridays. I don't remember what we did about holidays, but the solution must have been at least somewhat amenable.

When the bus arrived each day, we had kicked out our four lines in the gravel driveway to mark and secure our appropriate places, and order in society had been preserved for another day. Each of the four of us would go on to attain not only our high school diplomas but college degrees, as well. Who knows the destruction that our in fighting may have caused but for those lines in the gravel that allowed us to focus on lesser things like getting an education and making a positive difference in society.

Today, when we look back at the lines in the gravel, we laugh and wonder how we could have argued about something so trivial. Perhaps because that was one of many more situations in the years to come that proved to each of us that the world did not revolve around any one of us. Today, "Lines in the Gravel" is just one of many often re-told childhood stories, one in which we recall how we learned to live at peace with one another.

conversations with Smokie's owners, Mom also discovered that we were safeguarding a star. One of the local banks had been shooting a commercial at one of the parks where Smokie and his owners happened to be visiting on that particular day. As they were filming, Smokie ran across the shot, well in the background. Even after the commercial was later edited, Smokie's cameo remained. We returned Smokie to his grateful owners that day but rushed to the TV every time one of us announced, "Smokie's on TV!!!"

Smokie's owners called us not too long afterward with an offer we could not refuse. They had some German shepherd-mix puppies, and they wanted us to have one. He was the cutest little fella that our pastor said looked like a Teddy bear, so we named him Teddy. Though he was a mixed breed, Dad felt he should have a name befitting a full breed, so he "officially" became Mortimer Theodore Snerd. Sometimes referred to by Dad as Ol' Mort, Teddy grew up to be an expert car chaser. I suppose our road would have come to resemble a junkyard had he not chased all those cars away.

Mom, however, never really warmed up to Teddy. He bit Mama Tomp once, and I don't think Mom ever forgave him for that. Though Teddy was the family dog that we kids would most associate with our childhood, he wasn't loved equally by all of us. The divide between Mom and Teddy would soon worsen.

It started with an unexpected call from Smokie's owners. They were moving and would not be able to take Smokie with them. Well, of course we would love to have him! (Okay, the response wasn't that immediate, but, nevertheless, he came to live with us.) We were all glad to have him back, and Teddy was glad to have a canine playmate.

Teddy began to show Smokie the ropes of being an Ainsworth family dog. Unfortunately, as it turned out, this included the role of serving the family by chasing all the cars away. To hear Mom tell the story, Smokie was better at car-chasing than Teddy; he actually caught one. Smokie gave his life one day in the line of duty while his younger but more experienced mentor lived to chase cars for many more years to come.

If Teddy could not overcome a little bite on the leg of her mother, then Mom would be even more unforgiving of his being an accomplice in the death of her favorite dog. So, for the rest of his days with us, Teddy was a mutt in a quite different way: five-sixths family dog, beloved pet, and marker of our childhood; and one-sixth conniver and villain.

20 CORN FLAKES AT MIDNIGHT

My mother's parents were Wilson and Wilma Thompson. I share my grandfather's middle name, Wade. We simply knew them as Tomp and Mama Tomp. When my sisters and brothers and I were young, my parents would drive us two hours north from Star to North Carrollton, where they lived, to spend a week with Tomp and Mama Tomp. We only saw them a couple of times during the rest of the year, just for part of a day each time, so we looked forward to our week in North Carrollton each year.

The drives to Tomp and Mama Tomp's were adventures enough in those days before mandatory seatbelt laws. I remember the six of us piling into the two-door '69 Ford pickup truck (yes, all six of us); watch out if you were just to Dad's right as he shifted through the gears. I remember the '75 Gran Torino (Dad, how fast are you going?) that allowed us to stretch out a little bit and the two-tone green Dodge van that I don't really remember much about except that it sorta reminded me of the Mystery Machine from Scooby Doo. Finally, there was the '81 Corolla, the one in which Andy (since he was the youngest) had to ride on the emergency brake between the two front bucket seats. Sure, he had a pillow to sit on, but it *was* a two-hour drive. Bless his heart.

During our week with Tomp and Mama Tomp every summer, I rarely remember our driving anywhere. Mama Tomp didn't drive at all, and Tomp drove only on rare occasions. So we walked everywhere.

We walked out their back door to the railroad tracks, less than 50 yards away, and walked along the rails. We walked maybe a quarter of a mile or so to the railroad trestle and walked across it. That was fun since we didn't have a railroad trestle to cross in Star.

We walked about the same distance in the other direction to the general store, the store with bottled drinks on ice in enormous troughs. There's nothing like an ice-cold grape drink from a bottle. That was Nehi heaven.

We walked to Mama Tomp's friends' houses. There, we were expected to sing Mama Tomp's favorite hymns to her friends. Seems like "Trust and Obey" was her favorite—good words to live by. We were regularly commended for our singing, but they were just being polite, as we would rudely discover back in our hometown in our teenage years.

Finally, if Tomp was feeling up to it, we would walk to the big bridge that separated North Carrollton from Carrollton (an important distinction among the locals for reasons I never did discover). The big bridge was probably a mile-and-a-half, maybe two miles, away from their house, and the Jitney Junior was conveniently positioned on the way back. (It was, after all, a *convenience* store.)

Once during every week of summer spent at my grandparents', Mama Tomp would fry up some scrumptious hamburgers. I don't know what she did to those things, but they were *sooommmme* good. When they were ready to serve, she would fold a paper towel in half, place it over half the burger, wrap it underneath, and tuck the edges so that we held in our hands a restaurant-quality burger both by taste and presentation.

The most memorable taste of every summer trip for us, however, was not those burgers but Corn Flakes. Near the end of our week every year, Tomp and Mama Tomp would let us stay up until midnight, which was about the time the train rolled through. Every year, Mama Tomp would pour us a bowl of Corn Flakes (with a spoonful or two of sugar that sweetened the milk nicely) to enjoy as we opened the back door and watched the train roar by. I remember the sheer power of the train in its close proximity to us. The house literally rattled, and we always wondered how we remained asleep on all the other nights we spent there.

I lament that on one of our summer trips, Mama Tomp and I got our wires crossed about my chore of sweeping off that dadgum front porch a dozen times a day. That's when our carefree weeks in North Carrollton ceased. When I think back on those days now, I remember fondly ice-cold Nehi grapes, walks to the big bridge, and restaurant-quality hamburgers. And Corn Flakes at midnight. As an avid fan of The Andy Griffith Show, I recall these summertime visits to Tomp and Mama Tomp's as my little slice of Mayberry.

21 THE UNINHIBITED JOY OF A ROMP IN THE MUD

The carefree days of our childhood could be symbolized by many icons. A dusty old field where I developed a passion for the game of baseball. A quilted pallet in the yard under the oak trees with a book in every Ainsworth kid's hands. The brown Bookmobile in the parking lot of the Baptist church on Wednesday afternoons. Pop and Granny's front porch. The back walkway that we kids would leap as we raced in opposite directions around Tomp and Mama Tomp's house. The fellowship hall during family night suppers at church. I have so many reminders of an idyllic childhood, all of which trigger warm memories of days gone by. One little patch of mud, though, tops them all.

When I think of the unhindered, uninhibited joys of childhood, no single experience captures the thought more for me than the day I slipped in the mud. Lu Ann recalled that it happened on an Easter afternoon after a recent rain. Already in my everyday clothes after church, I was walking across the yard for who-knows-what reason when I encountered a particularly slippery patch of ground near the water faucet. I went down in an instant, covered in mud from head to toe. My sisters and brother soon "slipped" in that same spot after me, and without initial permission from Mom and Dad, we spent the next few hours running and sliding in our ever-expanding mud hole.

With nearly 20 years experience as a parent myself now, I know that parents spend the better part of their kids' childhood saying *no*. One would expect anything leading to the sloppification of clothes to fall squarely in the category of *no*. On the day of the blissful mud hole romp, though, our expected *NO* never happened. Instead, my parents simply shook their heads and smiled as they watched us, their lack of intervention as close to a *yes* as we needed that afternoon.

I suppose the massive cleanup to follow was worth the trouble for my mother. What's an extra load of laundry compared to the blissful joy of childhood? Mom hadn't had brothers and sisters with whom to play, and she had determined that we would. This was her desire come to life, though it may have been just a shade messier that she had envisioned.

One time, when my older two kids were about the same age as I was during my childhood mud slide, they were playing outside with the Baker boys from down the street when, suddenly, one of them slipped and fell in the mud. They all came to the door and asked permission for all of them to play in the mud. Both moms looked at me for the decision. Decisively and without hesitation, I answered, "Absolutely!" as I turned to get the camera.

22 CHURCH ADVENTURES

Our family attended the Wesleyanna United Methodist Church in Star. Most of the people we knew were either Baptists or Methodists since we really only had two choices in our little town. I had heard of Presbyterians and Episcopalians and Pentecostals and Seventh Day Adventists and so forth, but until I was in at least junior high school, I probably couldn't have named one. Church was a regular part of our lives, and it was about as predictable as anything else in a small Mississippi town like ours.

Wesleyanna, which is now over 165 years old, is a pretty little natural-stone building with an extremely steep-pitched roof over the sanctuary. It sits on a modest rise just off the southbound side of Highway 49, facing northbound traffic. The sanctuary itself is fairly small, with two equal sections of about 10-12 rows each, and most regular attenders have sat in the same location for quite some years. In all the years that we attended church together, I never remember sitting with the left-side families like the Mangums, Phillipses, and Clarks.

My family was a right-side family who always sat in the same pew, a couple of rows from the back. Mr. John and Ms. Myrtle Mayo always sat behind us on the very back row. Mr. John was usually one of the last men in from the pre-service, er, prayer meeting just outside the building. (And let me tell you, they were breathing fire at those prayer meetings....) Mr. John was like the anchor that held the back part of the church steady, always in the seat nearest the door. Ms. Myrtle, as sweet a lady as you could ever meet, was always about a word or two behind on the Apostle's Creed. I was convinced that the breaks between sentences were designed for Ms. Myrtle to catch up with the rest of us.

Mr. John and Ms. Myrtle were like so many other things in a small town like Star: dependable, consistent, and even predictable. Many other elements of our church fell under this description, as well. One of the regular events at our church was family night suppers every fifth Sunday. We could count on the same ladies bringing the same dishes every time. (After all, those same dishes were complimented last time.) To bring a different dish might just throw off the groove of the whole family night supper. My mom always took potato salad and deviled eggs. To this day, I haven't tasted a deviled egg as tasty as hers.

Family night suppers meant games for the kids as soon as we were finished eating. We rarely came prepared for games, but we would always make do. I remember rummaging through the church closets on more than one occasion to find a stray sock or even a wad of paper and some tape. A broom handle later and a game of tape ball was on. On some of the rougher nights, we played a variation of football (though not necessarily *with* a real football) whose name would cause it to be shut down on account of political incorrectness today. We found that the greatest resource we had for games at family night suppers was our imaginations.

During the year several events regularly dotted our church calendar. Summer time meant vacation Bible school and revival. During our weeklong revival services, we would actually use the small, soft-cover *Power and Praise* hymnals that sat in the back of the pews alongside our much larger hardback Methodist hymnals. I always enjoyed singing some of the "Baptist" hymns out of the *Power and Praise* and secretly wished that we used them more than just that week out of the year. During one of those revival services one summer when I was about ten years old or so, I clearly understood what salvation meant for the first time. As we stood there singing "Just As I Am" (which we only sang during revival), I knew I needed to walk to the front and find out what I needed to do to give my life to Jesus. But I didn't. The tugging on my soul wouldn't come again for almost another decade.

Another event on the Wesleyanna yearly calendar was the annual Thanksgiving service with the Baptist church on the Wednesday night prior to Thanksgiving. We rotated churches and pastors for this service, with the Baptist pastor preaching at our church one year and our pastor preaching at their church the following year. That's the service in which my family's harmonial deficiencies would be publicly ridiculed, but that's another story in itself.

Because of the predictability of going to church where we did, the wild cards drew particular attention. For our family, Andy was the wild card. Though Dad warned him every week that if he didn't behave that they were going to come home and "go round and round," Andy never could seem to keep it together for a whole two hours through Sunday school and church. He would find some way to misbehave, and Dad's belt would chase Andy around in circles until he got the message. Only, he was a little slow in getting the message.

Andy was also averse to smiling at us whenever he did anything in front of the church. Even as young teenagers, we were allowed to serve as ushers, passing the plates and collecting the tithes and offerings. When Andy served in this serious capacity, he would avoid eye contact with us as long as possible because he knew that we could break him down without even trying (though I am not admitting that we ever attempted to coerce a grin from him). He would go so far as to suck in his lips in a kind of reverse pucker, but a chuckle always forced itself through. Even as an adult, Andy is prone to smile a'plenty – not a bad characteristic, if you ask me. In those days, though, he tried to avoid any semblance of taking his public church duties lightly.

Ms. Diann Lee and my cousins John Earl and Scott sat a row or two in front of us. A couple of years younger than me (Wilagene's age), John Earl was a regular source of hijinks, as well. This was the cousin who knocked his front two teeth out at about eight years old shooting a double barrel 12-gauge shotgun (not at church, just to be clear). He also tore his leg wide open when his motorcycle didn't quite make it to the top of the hill at the sand pit one day.

One particular memory I have of John Earl in church—a far less injurious occasion than the aforementioned ones— was when he was a little fella. John Earl's attention was easily lost once the children's sermon had taken place and all the kids had returned to their seats to sit quietly and still with their parents during the main sermon. Never being one for much quiet and still, on this occasion, John Earl decided to go exploring. Slipping down from his seat without notice, he began to crawl around on the floor. Seeing that he was garnering the attention of everyone on the back three or four rows of the right side of the sanctuary, he began to make his way toward the front, parting legs as necessary on his journey forward.

The preacher continued on with his message, perhaps unaware that he was losing the battle for the concentration of the people at his left to a little rug rat now nearing the end of his journey. John Earl made his way past the last set of legs and continued on another row. I'm sure Ms. Diann was mortified, but it was too late to snag him now without causing a major distraction as this had gone on for several minutes by this point.

The attention of everyone on our side was riveted on what John Earl would do next. Would he continue past the empty front pews and come out right in front of the preacher? Would he attempt an escape through the front door? No, John Earl was never a child to escape the spotlight. Knowing that he had an eager audience behind him, John Earl chose the first empty pew to turn around, pop up, and heartily wave to all his adoring fans.

The kids all giggled out loud. The adults snickered with their that-was-cute-but-I'm-an-adult-and-I-was-really-trying-to-concentrate-on-this-important-sermon laughs. I don't remember what Ms. Diann did with him. She may have gone round and round with John Earl when they got home. All I know is that every once in a while, one of us Ainsworth kids will re-tell an old story that starts with, "Remember the time John Earl..." And that usually leads to, "Remember when Andy..." And we all go back to a simple time when our parents and our church were trying to teach us right from wrong. In the process we learned an unintended lesson: we learned how to live in community with others...even the wild cards.

23 TEDDY AND THE HOT DOG

The family dog associated with my childhood was Teddy, the German shepherd, cocker spaniel, Labrador retriever mix. Sure there were other dogs, but he was the one who was there through most of my formative years.

Teddy was generally good-natured, but he was the only dog of ours that I remember who would occasionally bite someone. He bit Mama Tomp once when she and Tomp had come down from North Carrollton for a visit. He went after my friend Sidney another time, sending him into a Dukes of Hazzard-ish slide across the hood of his brand-new Z-28. We laughed about that later...actually, I laughed while it was happening.

Teddy also vehemently hated a stuffed German shepherd with a realistic-looking plastic head that my sisters kept tucked away in their closet. Occasionally, we would pull that thing out and growl and make it lunge at Teddy. That would get him heated up, but that's not the "hot dog" story I remember most about Teddy.

It happened on a Saturday night. I know that it was a Saturday night because of the Ainsworth weekend routine. Every Friday night was hamburger night, and every Saturday night was hot dog night. Saturday night was also an opportunity for my sisters to demonstrate their creativity; they drew and spelled various messages with mustard on white bread as they prepared hot dogs for my dad, who often worked the midnight shift and was rarely off on Sundays, to take to work later that night or the next day.

Teddy fell into a routine on hot dog night, too. He might wander around under the table early on in the meal, hoping for a handout; Wilagene was especially generous, and Mom was particularly stingy with table scraps. However, when Dad reached the final bite of each of his two hot dogs, he could count on Teddy's being seated just to his right. Teddy knew that he owned that last bite, even if it occasionally contained some Old El Paso hot sauce. (Dad sometimes derived some sick pleasure at watching the poor dog sit there licking his lips for several minutes after each bite.)

Dad would naturally do a no-look hand-off—so as not to get "caught" by Mom—of the last bite to Teddy's waiting jaws. He was adept at avoiding Teddy's teeth as they made the exchange; there were a few botched passes, but they pretty much had it down to a routine...until the night that Teddy received a false signal.

Dad had just finished his first hot dog, and Teddy had gotten the last bite, as usual. Dad was launching into a pretty demonstrative story as he prepared his second hot dog. The hot dog was fixed and ready to eat and in Dad's right hand as he entered a particularly animated part of the story. He spread his arms wide to illustrate some salient point, and I saw it coming; his right hand (with the whole hot dog still in it) was perfectly positioned directly in front of Teddy's snout. As they had practiced every Saturday night for so many weeks prior, Teddy naturally took what was offered to him.

Dad froze in the middle of his story, turned to the dog who had in one swift move inhaled the hot dog, and said, "Why, you...." (I'm not leaving out an expletive, by the way; Dad didn't talk like that, at least not in front of us.) Before he could get angry at the dog, I think he realized what his move must have looked like to Teddy, so Dad decided to let him enjoy his moment, not to mention his whole hot dog. We all laughed as Teddy innocently looked up at

Dad as if to say, "What?"

The next Saturday night, Teddy was right back in his place to enjoy the last bite of Dad's hot dogs. Dad, however, was always careful after that to be sure that Teddy only enjoyed the *last* bite.

24 DEVIL IN THE DITCH

One of the joys of childhood is unfettered imagination. Kids say and do the darnedest things...and make up the darnedest games. The Ainsworth kids were no exception.

Church was a great outlet for our imaginative games. Every week after church was over, the adults would stand around and talk. Some of the kids—and there must have been upwards of six or eight of us on a good week in our small church—would head outside to the southeast corner of the building for our weekly game of Devil in the Ditch. The four of us and our cousins John Earl and Scott were regulars.

The Wesleyanna United Methodist church building itself is a unique structure. Built from local sandstone back in the 1950's, the church's sanctuary has a high, pointed roof that from the outside belies the actual seating capacity of maybe 100 or so. A two-storied wing to the north contained Sunday school rooms and a fellowship hall. Pop helped build the church, and I understand that he and Granny attended together for a while. During my lifetime, though, I never actually knew Pop to go to church; by the time I came along, Granny had returned to her roots in the Baptist church, where she sang in the choir for most of my childhood years. My dad kept our family in the Methodist church.

The wall on the north side of the sanctuary was a normal

ground-to-roof structure, but the south side had a drainage system with what amounted to a concrete ditch running alongside the wall between support columns. Devil in the Ditch was played on the part of the ditch that was open on either side, with the church grounds on one side and the covered entryway on the other. With columns on either side of the ditch, the width of the play area was about eight feet, or about half the reach of a child. The object was to pass safely from one side to the other without being tagged. The "devil" was the kid unfortunate enough to have to stand in the ditch and attempt to tag passers-by.

The bigger kids had a distinct advantage, both as the "devil" and as those trying to avoid him. As the "devil," their more extensive reach helped them get out of the ditch more quickly by making a tag. Longer legs were a distinct advantage when crossing the ditch, as well. The bigger kids could get across with only one step in the ditch while the smaller kids took two steps in the ditch to cross. The game was at its peak of fun when we could get the "devil" moving in one direction with a good fake, allowing those on the opposite end to cross the ditch barely untagged. Then, we could get the "devil" going back and forth, narrowly averting tags on either side of the ditch.

Devil in the Ditch had no discernible moment in which the game was won or lost. Instead, we played until our parents had concluded their conversations and called us to leave. Too bad if you were "the devil" at that point, but the game would start anew the following Sunday.

The kids of this generation at Wesleyanna no longer have the after-church outlet of Devil in the Ditch. A number of years ago, the outer entry of the church was taken in as a foyer and balcony. The ditch is still there today, but if a kid were to try to cross it today, he would run smack into the outer wall of the foyer—not much fun in that, I suppose.

I also suppose that there's something glorious in the nostalgia of a made-up game that was only for a specific era, our era.

Perhaps there is the wider lesson, too, of taking advantage of the resources and opportunities we have in a given time, knowing that those resources and opportunities can so quickly change as time marches relentlessly on.

25 DAD'S MOTORCYCLE AND A BET WITH THE PREACHER

I have never known my dad to be much of a bettin' man. He is simply too fiscally conservative to spend his money on games of chance. More to the point, he's a tightwad. But there was this one time when he bet the Methodist preacher that his motorcycle would start on the first kick. This was a bet I had seen him make before, and he had won every time.

Dad's motorcycle was a 1971 three-cylinder, two-stroke Kawasaki 500. This was a much-ballyhooed bike from the motorcycle racing circuit. Several of Dad's friends had checked it out and concluded, "This is a bike that could hurt you." Coming off a motorcycle accident earlier in his life on another bike that had left him with a broken kneecap and that could have been much worse, my dad needed to hear those words. Though I was still in elementary school when he had the Kawasaki, I don't recall any recklessness on his part with that bike. What I do remember is that it always cranked on the first kick.

The Kawasaki was Dad's last motorcycle for a long time. As the four of us kids got older, Dad made a series of choices that we wouldn't realize the value of until we were adults. He knew that he couldn't be the father that he desired to be and continue to ride like he had in his days as a single man. Though he sold his bike, he never lost the urge to ride. In the following years, when we would ask him what he wanted for Father's Day, he would always respond, "A motorcycle."

One year, with Mom's help, we gave in and got him a motorcycle. It was a beautiful metallic greenish-blue not too far from the color of his Kawasaki 500. He treasured that motorcycle, keeping it on display in its little case on top of his chest of drawers. He also stopped asking for a motorcycle.

When my oldest two children were about the age I was when Dad bet the Methodist preacher, I faced a similar choice. For me, the time thief was golf. After too many Saturday mornings chasing the wayward little ball around, I decided the game was not worth what it was costing me (though I generally did take more shots for my money than did most of my friends). I did not have the money or the time to be proficient at golf, and my children were growing up at home without me. That was the point in my life when I began to understand some of the sacrifices my dad had made to build a legacy of priority on family.

When my dad retired after many years as a trailer mechanic, Mom bought him a real motorcycle, a Honda Shadow. He began to ride again after almost 30 years away from motorcycles. Well into his 70's now, Dad still rides occasionally.

A few innovations in motorcycles had occurred over those three motorcycle-less decades, one of which was electronic ignition. Electronic ignition is probably more expensive than an old school kick starter, but it may have been good for my dad's wallet anyway. You see, all those years before, Brother Roger had won that bet.

26 TWENTY-FIVE RED CHRISTMAS RIBBONS (OR LINES IN THE GRAVEL REVISITED)

My mom had helped our family avert meltdown over how we kids lined up to wait for the bus with her chart and our lines in the gravel. I suppose, then, that we should have felt guilty that our sibling rivalry issues flared up again every December. A mother who stays home with her children through their formative years should expect much more from her children, right? (Don't answer that. I have lived it from the other side of the coin now. Not as a stay-at-home mom, for the record, but as the husband of one.)

My mom loved to cross-stitch. We had her works of art all over the house. One that hung in my boyhood room and now hangs in the cabin just over the hill from their house reads:

A great gray elephant
A little yellow bee
A tiny purple violet
A tall green tree
A red and white sailboat
On a blue sea
All these things you gave to me
When you made my eyes to see
Thank you, God!

I have since learned that the origin of that little poem was in a Little Golden Book called *Prayers for Children*. Then, I just knew that Mom spent a great deal of time and effort cross-stitching it just for me.

Another of Mom's cross stitch works, the most memorable of all of them, was brought out at the end of every November and was the source of our lines in the gravel revisit. I remember its white background but neither I nor any other member of my family can tell you from memory what words are stitched onto said background. We could, though, tell you all about the little plastic rings, numbered one through twenty-five, and the small red ribbons tied to each of them.

This was our countdown to Christmas. Each night our family would gather during the preceding 24 days, and one of us would untie a ribbon commemorating the passing of another day. Therein lay a problem, however: only **one** of us could untie a ribbon each day. Mom and Dad did not take a turn, but an eternity seemed to pass between turns for each of us. Gosh, Christmas came slowly enough already. The ribbons just seemed to heighten our awareness of how slowly time was moving (at least until only a few ribbons remained). When we had to wait through the other three turns to take down another ribbon, it was almost more than a hyper-competitive, ultra-anxious little soul could endure.

You can do the math of four kids and 25 Christmas ribbons and predict the eventual dilemma. The twenty-four days leading up to Christmas could be easily divided among our spirited foursome (though the order we established was not as easily settled upon – day to day or year to year). However, who would get to untie the Christmas Day ribbon was quite another issue. To wait four days during December to untie a ribbon was trying enough; to wait four years between turns of untying the Christmas Day ribbon was simply beyond our individual constraints.

Funny thing is, all six of us Ainsworths remember the "lines in the gravel" difficulty in some detail. But none of us remember how we worked out the Christmas ribbon rotation, only that we did. We evidently reached an amicable solution at some point. Perhaps we had learned something about taking turns by our difficulties in waiting on the school bus; whatever the reason, everyone's memories of the Christmas ribbons revolve around the tradition of doing it and the excitement that it generated in our whole family.

I talked to Dad a couple of weeks into the Christmas season (which starts *after* Thanksgiving, people!) last year and asked him about the Christmas ribbons. He said that yes, they were still around. He told me that with just he and Mom in their house now, they often forget to remove the ribbons for days at a time and that he had not yet even put it on the wall.

When he said that, I could almost feel the collective breath being sucked out of specific pockets of Mississippi, Alabama, and Oklahoma. We may have argued as children about whose turn it was to remove the ribbon on a particular day, but **never, never** were the Christmas ribbons forgotten. That was and is unthinkable—so much so, in fact, that this past Christmas, my family of five became the proud new caretakers of the Christmas cross-stitch and its accompanying 25 red ribbons.

27 A CUP OF COFFEE WITH MY MAMA

Dad worked as a trailer mechanic at Fruehauf Incorporated during our early childhood before going to work at Yellow Freight Systems. I like to say that the move to Yellow Freight took us from Toughskins to Levis. Financially, it opened up more possibilities for our family, but it also meant that Dad had to work evening or midnight shifts until he gained enough seniority to move to a shift more conducive to family life. It meant irregular sleeping schedules for him and accompanying changes in our daily routine. It meant his working on the weekends, which meant that he was seldom able to accompany us to church for a while. It also meant his working during some of our school and sports activities.

Dad's job change also brought a lengthy pause to a regular high point in the everyday routine for us children. Before Dad's job switch, he arrived home every day like clockwork. The four of us were always on the lookout at about the same time each day for Dad's truck. The pale green '69 Ford or, later, the red step-side Ford that he had bought from Uncle Cecil, would come into view through the front window of our dining area, and the four of us would race outside to meet him. With our agendas.

For Andy and me, Dad became the all-important third man for whatever sport was in season. Baseball season typically meant that Dad was the all-time pitcher in whatever modified baseball game we concocted. Football season meant a daily game of "three passes." Beginning at a utility pole in our back yard, our field went around a few scraggly trees into Uncle Cecil and Aunt Sissy's backyard past their grape trellises and into the end zone. We would rotate turns at quarterback and receiver and then count up all the touchdowns in which we were involved during a rotation to determine a winner. When basketball season rolled around, Dad was usually the *one* in a game of two-on-one, using his hook shot that he dubbed his *O.D. Philicrip* to take us down on a regular basis.

For Lu Ann and Wilagene, Dad became their trampoline partner. He also served as the official timer because his time had to be *exactly* evenly split between the two; my sisters were sticklers for equality when it came to trampolining and Dad's time. Any time they had learned a new trick on the trampoline, Dad had to watch with the appropriate level of interest before it counted. (I would experience this with my daughter years later at the swimming pool: "Daddy, watch me. Are you ready? Ready? Daddy, are you watching? Watch this!")

The race was on to Dad's truck every afternoon to determine whom he would play with first. His window was usually down as he pulled into the driveway, and he was met with a blast of "Daddywillyouplaywithmefirst?!?" as we each rushed to earn that day's preeminent spot in the play order. His response was always the same: "Let me have a cup of coffee with your mama first." We were left to argue with one another for the next little while about who had asked first and who went first yesterday and who had gotten the shaft the week prior...and wonder how a man who worked in the heat all day would want to come home and drink a hot cup of coffee anyway.

Sometimes Dad's "cup of coffee with our mama" took just a few minutes, and sometimes it took much longer, but he always eventually emerged from the house and played with us until dark. We wouldn't know the significance of that cup of coffee until years later. Back then, it was simply a temporary delay before our daily time with Dad.

For me, my moment of "cup of coffee with your mama" realization came when my daughter Ashton was not quite two years old. I had come home from a long day of teaching and coaching. Loretta was cooking supper, and it was about 30 minutes from being ready to eat. Our dining area was the only room in the house with carpet, and it was the perfect place that day to just collapse for a few minutes before our family supper. When I did, Ashton exploded into the room—all smiles and pent-up energy—and pounced on my back.

"Daddy, play with me!"

In an almost out-of-body experience, I heard myself saying to her, "Not now, sweetie. Daddy's too tired."

Even as the words came out of my mouth, I couldn't believe I was hearing myself say them. The years of Dad's regular routine with us came crashing in on me at that moment. I couldn't blame it on a job that was more stressful and tiring than his; I had spent a few months on two different occasions doing trailer mechanic work, coming home exhausted every day. And I only had one child then instead of four. *And* I wasn't even 30 years old yet. I had no excuse.

I peeled myself off the floor and played with my daughter that day. Two sons later, play seems like such a chore some days, and I still tap out way more often than I would like. I don't regret for one minute, though, being the rare dad who still gets out and plays with his kids because that's the example that was set for me.

I have also come to realize that Dad's "let me have a cup of coffee with your mama" was really communicating that their relationship was primary in our home. I must confess that I haven't done as well with the regularity of Dad's routine. However, my kids know what "let me have a cup of coffee with your mama" means, even though Loretta and I have only recently begun to drink coffee in the afternoon. The importance of making the marriage relationship foremost in the home didn't stop with my parents' generation, and we are determined that it won't stop with ours.

At the writing of this book, my parents are in their 70's and long since retired. The demands of their children have greatly subsided (though I will still call and announce that I have a "Dad" problem—one that I know he is bound to have some experience with—from time to time). Still, every day about three or four o'clock, Dad will look at their dog Biff and announce, "It's coffee time!" He and Mom will pour their cups of coffee, walk out to the swing in the gazebo if the weather is warm enough, and sit and talk. Occasionally, when I am in Star for a few days, I get to join them now.

28 MAMA BLUEBIRD

There is a photo of me somewhere at Mom and Dad's house from what I considered my best Christmas ever. I think I was 10 years old that year. Santa brought me a Minnesota Vikings Fran Tarkenton jersey that year, and I'm wearing it in the photo. Andy and I pored over the Sears Christmas catalog for hours every year before Christmas before finally choosing an NFL player jersey and an NFL team sweatshirt for that year. Over the years, I became Archie Manning, Ron Jaworski, Bert Jones, Roger Staubach, Ken Anderson – many of the great quarterbacks of that era.

In that same Christmas photo, I was holding the prize of that year's Christmas haul, my first BB gun. During the pre-Christmas conversations about my ability to handle a gun with some level of maturity, Mom had given me all of *The Christmas Story* warnings about being careful not to shoot my eye out. She was also insistent that I should never, ever shoot birds with it, either. Yeah, yeah, yeah, I had responded in my mind as I had given all the obligatory answers aloud.

I was more than ready to responsibly handle a BB gun. Too old to be getting my first BB gun, actually. My cousin John Earl was two years younger than I was and had already shot a double-barrel 12-gauge. (Never mind that he knocked two of his teeth out in the process.)

Christmas Day came and the new BB gun was indeed under the tree along with a treasure chest of ammo! I couldn't wait to slip on the new Tarkenton jersey and go shoot some targets. When the morning festivities were complete (including posing for that photo with my new gun), I headed outside to start plinking some cans from the fence posts—but only after another round of safety instructions from Mom.

I was completely content to assail the invading wave of aluminum cans that day and in the days and weeks that followed, keeping my family's fortress free from their tyranny. As wave after wave of the Aluminati surrendered to my proficient marksmanship, their kingdom weakened until they were no longer a potential danger to the Ainsworth domain. As with any warrior worth his salt, the boredom of having no battle to wage was a powerful, crippling force.

One day while on routine patrol, I noticed a mama bluebird perched on the limb of the giant pine tree in front of my dad's shop. A thought ran through my mind, the thought that has brought about the demise of many pre-teen boys through the generations, "I wonder what would happen if..." If you were to have asked me what I thought would happen in that moment, I couldn't have told you. All I know is that I raised my gun toward mama bluebird and squeezed the trigger. I absolutely did not expect her to plummet from her perch, never to fly or sing again. I stood aghast at this totally unanticipated state of affairs.

Don't shoot my eye out and don't shoot birds. Those were my only two instructions, and I had broken one of them within weeks of getting my first BB gun. I felt like my only choice was to cover it up, to keep it from Mom. Looking around and not seeing anyone nearby, I grabbed mama bluebird's tail with as little of my fingers as required to hold her and threw her lifeless body into the tall weeds near Aunt Sissy's garden next door.

Days passed, and the expected repercussions never came. I had gotten away with the perfect crime. Except...every time I saw a bluebird, I felt the guilt. The BB gun had certainly lost its luster. It's not easy being the only one carrying the guilt of killing an innocent mama bluebird, something I was specifically told not to do. So I did what I should have done the day it happened. I finally got up the nerve to tell Mom, and I told her what happened...last year, 37 years later.

I can finally look at that Christmas photo again, guilt assuaged, having learned a valuable lesson about trusting authority, about trusting that Mom did indeed know best.

29 THE PRICE OF BOILED PEANUTS

My dad would take a week of vacation from work every summer to work in the garden. I didn't really understand that then; to a kid, vacation meant that you went somewhere and did something fun so that your kids would have something exciting to write about when that inevitable "What I Did on Summer Vacation" writing assignment arrived in the fall. I understand the premise of Dad's choice much better now.

In my adult years, I have revived a fondness for gardening, one that was often lost in the heat of Star, Mississippi, summers. My garden today consists of a few raised beds used for growing tomatoes mostly. I have grown cantaloupes, watermelons, and squash, too, but my prolific blackberry vines have taken over two of the beds once used for growing other things. Dad's garden—our family garden—was much more extensive. Every year, the garden produced row after row of peas, butter beans, string beans, okra, squash, corn, and tomatoes. I also remember garden-grown carrots and radishes, at times.

We also grew peanuts one year, and two memories from that experience stand out vividly. I recall a fascination with just how much growth had taken place under the ground. Sure, I had pulled carrots and radishes from the ground by no more than the little sprig on top of the ground before, but the massive piles of peanuts that had grown so bountifully out of sight was impressive.

The second memory from our experience growing peanuts was equally impressive but not so much in a positive way. After we (and by *we*, I mean mostly Dad) pulled the peanuts from the ground, we brought the clusters near the house to wash them off and pull off the individual peanuts. We soon discovered, though, that we had evidently planted ants along with the peanuts. And not just ants—fire ants! They were everywhere! I remember not even being able to hold a cluster of peanuts to wash them off without being covered by those biting, stinging little critters.

We never planted peanuts again, so I guess the trauma of the fire ants wasn't limited to my little hands, arms, and legs. Too bad, because I love peanuts, especially boiled peanuts. After I began to drive a few years later, I discovered a wonderful place just up Highway 49, a place that I had passed for many years: Donna's #6 Produce. For a little more than a dollar then, I could get a pound of the tastiest boiled peanuts that you could imagine. Tasty boiled peanuts that did not come at the price of a week's worth of pain.

Donna's #6 Produce has become an icon on the Star landscape. It has grown from a little fruit stand on the side of the highway to a sizable operation with a large building that is almost always surrounded by the vehicles of its numerous customers. They sell almost every local fruit and vegetable that you could imagine, and they have even expanded their merchandise base beyond produce. (Hey, someone has to sell "Mississippi Girl" T-shirts in Faith Hill's hometown.)

For me, though, Donna's #6 Produce exists for one product and one product only. As a matter of fact, though Donna's is such a part of the fabric of Star, it is the only product I ever remember buying there. Boiled peanuts. The ant-free variety. Well worth the price.

30 GARDENIAS AND PERKER

When my sisters and brother and I were children, we played many games to keep ourselves entertained. Some were universal, like tag or hide and seek. Others were limited only to our imaginations. Perker was kind of an incorporation of both.

Uncle Hob, my dad's twin brother, and his wife, Evelyn, lived all the way across the county in Pelahatchie with their three kids, Beth, Susan, and Thom. (You may have heard the 1967 ballad "Ode to Billy Joe." We used to sing that Billy Joe McAllister jumped off the *Pela*hatchie, instead of the *Talla*hatchie, Bridge.) Though Pelahatchie was only about 45 minutes away from Star, we would only get together with the cousins a few times a year but always on Christmas Eve at Pop and Granny's house.

After Granny's feast of fish and oysters and the fixin's, the adults would gather in the living room to catch up, and the kids would head outside to play. The giant gardenia bush in the front yard always served as the gathering spot and as base. This was the gardenia bush that had been a fixture in the yard since Dad and Uncle Hob and Aunt Sissy had run around in the yard a generation before. To my dad, the scent of that gardenia bush is still what he considers the smell of summer. Perhaps the same bush functioned as base for them, too.

As the years went by, we outgrew hide and seek, and tag

morphed into the more complex freeze tag to the even more sophisticated Chinese freeze tag. One year, we didn't feel like playing any of the old stand-bys, so we decided to make up a new game. It was a conglomeration of all the other games of tag. Two tags and you were *it*. The rest of the rules are rather hazy now, but they seemed adequate at the time.

The most important element of our newly minted game of tag was giving it a unique name. Who knew but that it might gain international renown, and we had to be sure that it could be traced back to its originators. We settled on Perker. Perker was the name of one of our chickens, the white one who wouldn't lay eggs. This little factoid had no significance on our game, but it would have great impact on the chicken that would go on to gain infamy as our Thanksgiving dinner one year. (My wife has a firmly held belief that you shouldn't kill and eat any animal that you name, but my dad didn't know that rule back then...back when he wrung Perker's neck and had Mom serve her with giblet gravy. But I digress.)

My sisters and brother, the cousins, and I spent several Christmas Eves running around Pop and Granny's front yard yelling in sing-song voices, "Perker, Perker, Perker-Perker-Perker!" I don't think that was as much a rule of the game as it was a celebration of our creativity. On and on we would frolic until someone was inevitably unfairly treated beyond reconciliation and the game would be suspended until the following Christmas Eve.

At the home where my family now lives, I designed the landscape and filled it with a variety of flowers, plants, and bushes. Part of the overall theme of the landscape (besides making the mowing patterns as simple as possible) was to incorporate plants and flowers that came from friends and family. We have daylilies that came from a family that has been growing them for many years, azaleas that came from two different bushes nearly 40 years old, and one very special gardenia bush started from a piece of the one in Pop and Granny's front yard. Sometimes when I walk past it and breathe in its sweet fragrance, I imagine my dad as a kid running around and playing, and I can almost hear the carefree voices from my own childhood: "Perker, Perker, Perker-Perker-Perker!"

Though more than 200 miles separate me from where Pop and Granny's house used to stand, my gardenia bush is there to remind me every time I walk by it of a legacy of joy and happiness through at least four generations. Sometimes, after a harsh winter, I have to cut it back severely and I fear that I will lose the treasured bush. But it has always come back, time after time. The old bush still stands at Pop and Granny's old place, a reminder of summers long before I was born. And Perker.

31 WHEN STACY DILMORE PITCHED, WE HAD A CHANCE

Summer baseball in Star, Mississippi, brings back many memories. Like riding as a team in the back of pick-up trucks, trying our best to keep our caps from flying off our heads as we rode up Highway 49 to Florence or Plain (as Richland was then called—it was funny to play Plain Red or Plain Green or Plain Yellow) or down to Harrisville. Like remembering the era when wood bats gave way to the new aluminum ones. Like the coach or a parent treating us to ice cream after games that we won (and sometimes if we gave a great effort and sometimes, well, just because). Only after road games, though, because there was nowhere to buy soft-serve ice cream in Star.

The teams from Star played at Falcon Field, home of the (now defunct) Rankin Academy Falcons. The infield was all dirt, and there was no outfield fence. Unlike Florence's and Richland's teams, all the baseball and softball teams from Star—there was only one in each age group of our league—practiced and played on the same field. The stake-down bases and pitching rubber were moved to accommodate whichever team had the field at any particular time. The dugouts were minimal, and there certainly weren't any such frills as batting cages or bullpen mounds. The concession stand right behind the backstop was a tiny dark-green concrete-block building. (Once, one of the local residents broke in, popped some popcorn and poured a Coke, and left fifty cents, the appropriate price for those selections, on the counter.)

The uniforms for my team were white with red pinstripes—like a candy cane. In an unprecedented big-time move in Smalltown U.S.A. during the mid-seventies, one of the powers-that-were determined that we should have our names on the back of our uniforms. Well, the names weren't technically *on* the uniforms but on blocks on fabric that could be sewn onto and removed from the uniforms. And the names were our first names. As a long-time baseball aficionado now, I consider first names on the backs of jerseys rather bush league. Maybe it's because *Al* seemed an island on an ocean of fabric while *Ainsworth* would have certainly broadened my shoulders and taken my game to a whole 'nother level.

Whether through last names on our jerseys or perhaps an infusion of talent, we could have used something to propel our game to a more competitive level. We had good fundamental coaching through Coach Roland Walker and later through Coach Phil White and others, but we never managed to win more than a handful of games in any one season. The older team from Star wreaked fear in the hearts of opposing pitchers; it was fun to watch Plain's outfielders back up to the woods (no fence there, either), only to watch Johnny Williams hit the ball over their heads anyway. Our team, on the other hand, never managed to carry on that legacy of striking fear into the hearts of our opponents. In a day when trophies were won and not simply given to every participant, I remember receiving small trophies after a particularly successful season (by our standards) when we finished 5-9.

Very few of the guys I started playing baseball with when I was six years old were still around when we aged out of our Little League after age 12. Perhaps it was the transiency of the kids in our age group that diminished our potential for sustained success. One thing, however, stayed consistent through the years. When Stacy Dilmore pitched, we had a chance. Stacy was a year older than I, and he was that guy that you see on all the kid baseball movies, the star athlete among a gang of misfits. He threw hard enough to produce some strikeouts that ensured that the rest of us would not have to actually catch a fly ball or field a grounder and make an accurate throw to first. The more outs Stacy could procure via strikeout, the better our chances for success.

Stacy's parents, Eugene and Major Jean (pronounced locally as Ma-jean) Dilmore, were some of the most hospitable people that I have ever encountered. To eat supper with them was to encounter a multitude of requests to serve you more tea...or peas...or potatoes...or meat...or anything else that was on the table...or anything that wasn't on the table, for that matter. Mr. Dilmore, more commonly known to the adults as "Yogi," was a faucet of encouragement when Stacy was pitching. If Stacy was struggling to throw strikes, everybody knew what was coming next: "Rock and fire, Stacy, rock and fire! Just you and the mitt, you and the mitt. Forget about the batter, just rock and fire!"

Some of us who grew up playing on the old red-dirt Falcon Field found surprising success at brand-new McLaurin High School while Stacy Dilmore had already established himself at neighboring Florence High School. While I was never what you would call a prolific hitter, either in Little League or in high school, one potential moment of glory for me came in a game against Florence. Two outs, runner on second, tie game, and who else but Stacy Dilmore on the mound for the Eagles. I fouled off several pitches and then—smack! —a base hit to right, quite possibly the only base hit I ever had off a curve ball, a potential game winning hit, and off Stacy Dilmore, to boot! Alas, Billy Joe Walker got a late break from second base and only made it to third. The next batter made an out, and we lost in extra innings.

I'm not bitter, mind you. Even with Stacy Dilmore pitching, we had had our chance.

32 JOCK

The Nortons lived over the hill from us. The paved road ended just past their house, and we never had much reason to go that direction. They had a dog, though, that decided he wanted to live with us. The dog was mostly black, a mutt who was maybe part collie. He just showed up one day and acted like he belonged. I believe that Dad reported the missing canine to the Nortons, but they didn't seem to care where their dog took up residence. Dad tried to run him off, but for whatever reason, he chose to stay with us.

There were a couple of reasons the Nortons' dog probably chose to stay with us more than a day or two: first, we fed him and, second, we named him. I don't remember why, but we named him Jock, and he became part of our animal entourage, Teddy's sidekick. Every day, Dad still told Jock to go on back home but with no success. Sometimes, he even walked him back over the hill to the Nortons' house, but Jock always followed him back home.

Dad was a longtime animal lover, especially dogs, but he never really took to Jock. Deep down, we knew he wasn't really our dog but an interloper. However, there was something about being chosen that endeared ol' Jock to the rest of us.

One day, Jock took sick. Really sick, like about-to-die sick. Dad called the Nortons and suggested that Jock (or whatever his name was in his former life) might do well with a trip to the vet. They were indifferent toward Jock's predicament, but we kids insisted that *something* had to be done for the poor guy.

I remember thinking that Dad was softening his stance toward Jock when he placed Jock's limp and practically lifeless body in the back of an old long-wheel-base Chevy truck with a camper top that we had. He put some old blankets around Jock to make him as comfortable as possible. Eventually, as Jock clung to life, Dad moved him up to Uncle Cecil's barn. At least that way, Jock didn't have to die out there where any of us could discover him. Dad went to check on him every day and tried to get him to eat and drink but to no avail.

After about a week or so, Dad came back from the barn with some news. We had been expecting the news of Jock's death any day, but Dad reported that Jock was up and moving around a little and had eaten a little food and drunk some water. We were ecstatic! Dad had nursed him back from the brink of death and in doing so, shown a glimpse of compassion toward him.

Jock eventually made a full recovery. He got a few days' reprieve from Dad's admonishments to go back home to the Nortons, but ultimately, Dad returned to his daily practice of pointing down the road and telling Jock to just go on home.

One day, to everyone's shock, Jock went home. To hear Dad tell it, he simply pointed down the road and told Jock to go home, and Jock began walking home—simple as that. That didn't seem to Dad at all incompatible with the previous couple of *years* of his telling the dog the same thing every day without Jock's going home. But on this day, Jock had gone home. And he never came back.

Occasionally, throughout the years that followed, I would walk down the road for one reason or another. And there, right at the edge of the Nortons' yard, stood Jock (or whatever name they called him). It was always rather bizarre to walk past this dog who had not been ours and then been ours and now was not ours again.

I would look at him and say, "Hey, Jock," and he would return a knowing glance, as if to say, "'Sup. I remember you." I would then walk back over the hill to our house, and Jock would stay at the Nortons' house—as if it had always been that way.

33 THE HOWLING KID AT THE BAPTIST CHURCH

I don't know, maybe it was those weeks that we spent with Mama Tomp during the summer that led us to believe that we could sing. For the one week during the summer that we would spend with my maternal grandparents in North Carrollton, Mississippi, my sisters and brother and I became a traveling mini-choir. Our tour consisted of Mama Tomp's friends' houses around town. There were no roadies; our only equipment was our beautiful, melodic voices. I laugh at that notion. . . .

Tomp and Mama Tomp went to a Baptist church that sang some hymns that we rarely sang in our little Methodist church in Star, so we would have to brush up on her chosen songs when we arrived at their home each summer. Then, our mini-tour would begin. Day by day, we would go from home to home, singing Mama Tomp's favorite hymns.

Mama Tomp would introduce us at each stop, we would sing a few old stand-bys like "Standing on the Promises," and then we would take requests —usually hers, as I recall. She seemed very proud of us, and we sang to great reviews by our audiences. Only years later would we discover that they obviously did not have much to which they could compare us. Or that our voices changed tremendously during puberty. Or that our North Carrollton hosts were incredibly polite. Perhaps all three.

Unbeknownst to Mama Tomp, we were reluctant singers every step of the way. I do, however, remember shiny coins received at the close of many of those performances. Those shiny coins spent well on ice-cold Nehi grape sodas at the general store. So we sang.

Years went by, and I suppose the daily affirmations of our singing on these summer mini-choir mini-tours left me with a positive impression of our collective singing ability. True, I sang with the rest of my family week by week at our church, and the truth should have been apparent, but maybe the problem was with my ears and not with our voices.

The truth is, we sounded awful. Awwwwful! Don't take my word for it. Ask the sleeping kid at the Baptist church.

Once a year in our little town, the Wesleyanna United Methodist Church where my family attended would meet together with the Star Baptist Church for a Thanksgiving community service. On this particular year, the setting was the Baptist church in the sanctuary that burned to the ground a few years later. (That has no relevance to this story; it wasn't *that* bad.)

Our family must've gotten to the church early because we found seats near the back of the sanctuary. We sat a row behind a family from the Baptist church. Their little boy, a cute little fella about four or five years old as well as I can remember, was curled up asleep on their pew as the service began in the usual way with congregational songs of thanksgiving.

That's when it happened. The little lad in front of us—so cute and precious just moments before—sat bolt upright and turned around and stared incredulously at us. In a moment that stands frozen in my mind, he looked up and down the row at us as we sang—all the while with that stare of disbelief—and then flung his head back and howled. Yes, howled. At us! The mini-choir so well received in the North Carrollton circuit just a few years prior. Oh, the gall, the (only somewhat) unmitigated gall of this kid! His brash assessment was accurate, mind you, but his evaluative technique left much to be desired.

I thought of that kid often in my adult years, especially the 14 adult years that I spent *in my church choir*. I sang a couple of times a week at our church services. I sang at multiple Christmas musicals, some of them with famous people headlining. I sang at events for which our choir—and no other choir—was specifically invited. Heck, I even sang with the Brooklyn Tabernacle Choir. I'm not usually prone to brag much but. . . HA! Take that, howling kid. You put enough melodic voices around me, and this Ainsworth can sing!

34 CHUBS, HIS SIDEKICK, AND THE CORNBREAD INCIDENT

Chubs was probably the muttiest mutt we ever had. He was handsomely reddish in color with plenty of black and white mixed in. He was named for his plumpness in puppihood that soon gave way to a sleek, athletic build. Subject as all the humans and animals in our home were to Dad's proclivity to bestow multiple names, Chubs was also known as Chubby, Chubby Dog, Ol' Chubs, Chubby Ol' Groundhog, and "that big ol' boner boof dog."

Chubs's friendly nature won him many friends among people and pets alike. To no one, human or canine, was Chubs's cheery demeanor more attractive than to Uncle Cecil's dog Smokie. Smokie was a little beagle mix who adored Chubs, so much so that he began to follow Chubs around everywhere he went. Smokie was a smallish, mild-tempered little pup whose shadowing of Chubs always reminded me of Boo Boo following Yogi Bear.

Every evening at mealtime for Chubs, Dad would call out, "Come on, Chubs. Come get your clam chowder!" (No, we did not feed our animals gourmet meals; *clam chowder* was just another Abboism.) Smokie would follow Chubs to his bowl but patiently wait for Chubs to finish his meal...at least in the beginning. Smokie eventually helped himself to some of Chubs's leftovers, and though he was run off at first, he was just too stinkin' cute in his role as

Chubs's understudy to run off for good.

One day, I had gone over the hill to Pop and Granny's house. Smokie had followed me while Chubs was attending to some other matters at our house. Granny had just cleaned up the kitchen and had a couple of pieces of cornbread to throw out, so Smokie was to be the lone beneficiary of this good fortune. When she tossed the cornbread out into the yard, he eagerly ran to one piece and began to sniff. He looked curiously around and then picked up the piece of cornbread and ran off with it as if another dog was hot on his heels to take it away from him. He disappeared over the hill only to return—cornbread-less—a few minutes later to calmly lie down and enjoy the remaining cornbread. Granny and I learned later from those who had been at our house that when Smokie ran away with the first piece of cornbread, he had run to our house and dropped it in front of Chubs before returning to eat his own cornbread.

Everyone on the hill, including Uncle Cecil, was aware of the special fondness that Smokie had for Chubs. Eventually, we rarely saw Chubs without his sidekick. The only time that they were separated was at the end of the day, when Smokie would saunter next door to turn in for the night. That, too, would soon change. One afternoon, Uncle Cecil was walking by where Smokie slept, and he noticed that Smokie was tugging on his blanket. He simply looked at him and asked, "You moving out?" He was, indeed, completing the move to our house that he had been making progressively over the prior few months. He dragged his blanket to our house, cementing his position as the junior partner to Ol' Chubs.

As I remember Chubs and his little sidekick, I wonder how many of us are ever blessed to have a friend as loyal as Smokie was to Chubs. More importantly, I wonder how many of us set our own desires aside for the good of others like he did. You know, we can learn a lot from a little beagle.

35 CIGARETTES IN THE TEEPEE

When I was in seventh grade, I encountered peer pressure suddenly and with very little warning. It all started when I spent one Friday night at a new classmate's house. Jeff's dad and my dad had been friends in school, so my parents thought everything would be fine with my spending time at their house. They probably would have been right, too, if we had actually stayed in the house. Instead, we decided to be adventurous and sleep in the camper in the back yard. Throw in Jeff's neighbor Pat and a pack of cigarettes, and I was facing more than I had bargained for. I wanted to fit in, so I joined them in smoking a few that night.

I suppose I thought that I was not only cool at that point but that I was also then a smoker. Dad quit smoking over 30 years ago, but at that time, he had a two-packs-a-day habit. I swiped a pack of his cigarettes and some kitchen matches to feed my new habit. I would steal out behind Dad's shop for a smoke when no one else was home (not very often in a household of six). My hiding place for the cigarettes was just inside one of Dad's sheds, against the wall and out of sight.

Now, you might get the idea that just to the side of a door of a shed was a bad place to hide contraband, but you have to know my parents. They were post-Depression kids who watched their parents struggle to make it through those lean years; as a result, they are very reluctant to throw anything away. Now, I wouldn't classify them as hoarders, but they have numerous rooms and an increasing number of sheds full of stuff that the rest of us would have thrown away years ago. Maybe Dad was serious about "throwing a roof over the whole 28 acres and being done with it."

Back when I was a smoker, there were several outbuildings available from which to choose as a hiding place for "my" cigarettes: Dad's shop, the air compressor room attached to the shop, a small metal building with sliding doors behind the house, the 4-House (a open-front shed with a large number *4* painted on one of the sheets of plywood), and the teepee shed (a small A-frame outpost near the shop). The shop and air compressor room were definitely out as Dad was a regular in both of them. Nobody frequented the metal shed, but it was right behind the house and its doors made too much noise—too conspicuous. The 4-House's open front was too much of a risk for someone's stumbling upon my stash. The teepee shed was small, unlit, and rarely used. I figured it would be the best hiding place for "my" Viceroys.

The cool factor of sneaking stolen smokes alone behind the shop wore off pretty quickly. However, I was in too deep now; I *was* a smoker, after all. One day, as I should have anticipated, the gig was up. Dad called me out to the teepee shed, showed me the cigarettes and matches he had come across, and asked me if they were mine. I suppose I could have truthfully told him *no*; to be exact, the cigarettes were his and the kitchen matches were Mom's. I knew better than to try to slide on a technicality, though, so I 'fessed up.

To my shock and great pleasure, Dad did not appear to be angry with me, as I had expected. He just nodded and seemed glad just to have identified the culprit. Then, in what had to be one of his riskiest moments ever as a parent, he suggested we light up and smoke one together since I was a smoker.

I never saw it coming. He had started smoking when he was about 13, so I figured this was simply a coming-of-age ritual. Right out there by the teepee shed, I took a cigarette, exhibited a proficiency in lighting it, took a deep drag...and exhaled. I discovered that that was precisely the moment for which Dad was waiting.

"No, boy, if you're gonna smoke it, smoke it right. Inhale!"

Inhale?!? Wait, that wasn't part of the deal. I was just a boy; I couldn't be expected to smoke like a grown man, could I? In that moment of creative parenting on the part of my dad, my identity as a smoker was gone more quickly than the puff of smoke that was still rising toward the sky. Though I must confess that I smoked a stray cigarette from time to time over the next few years before promising my lungs a poison-free life, I never again considered myself a smoker, no matter how many cool points that distinction may have been worth.

36 THE LITTLE DIRT BASKETBALL COURT

My dad made an investment when I was still in elementary school that produced one of the best returns he ever enjoyed. No, basketball didn't pay for our college educations or anything like that (though my basketball career did produce a point on one-of-four free throw shooting on my ninth grade basketball team). The goal did highlight Dad's resourcefulness in supporting a family of six. A cut-off creosote pole and a piece of aluminum-coated trailer door that he salvaged from his job at Fruehauf formed the framework for our "brand new" basketball goal. He added a goal and a net, and we were in business.

I can't even begin to imagine the number of hours of enjoyment our basketball court produced. The court was located to the left of our house, facing my parents' and my sisters' bedroom windows. Even our driveway at that time was gravel, so no location would have given us the luxury of a smooth or level surface. By the time our basketballs had pounded the dirt a few hundred thousand times, though, the court was at least as *hard* as concrete, just not level.

The roots from the pine trees behind and to the left of the court made their appearance between the left wing and the left block. I would not learn to dribble effectively with my left hand until much later in life when I had regular access to a gym. The right side of the court was smoother but dropped off slightly in that direction. Though certainly not perfect, this new athletic venue would be the crown jewel of our sporting facilities for years to come. (It's all in the comparison, you see; compared to the badminton complex—basically, the clothesline—the basketball court was downright spectacular.)

Though the piece of trailer door served as a worthy backboard, the rim never seemed to stay attached for more than a few months at a time. This was more of an opportunity than a problem, as it turned out, thanks to the good folks at Kellogg's. The makers of Frosted Flakes—in exchange for an appropriate number of box tops—had the perfect remedy for a rimless backboard. A hard rubber baseball—official size, official weight.

I logged a substantial number of innings throwing to a self-determined strike zone, the area where the box on a store-bought backboard would have been. The *thonk, thonk, thonk* of ball hitting backboard must have driven my parents and sisters nuts when they were in their rooms during one of my countless imaginary games.

When I was not pitching on my imaginary team, I would often play infield, tossing the ball with a little less velocity against the backboard to produce a ground ball so that I could field it and fire across to first for the out. I was able to accomplish all this while not leaving an area of about three square feet just in front of the outside wall of Mom and Dad's room.

Occasionally, my imaginary coach would send me to the outfield for a game or two. I could produce a fly ball by dropping down to a lower angle and throwing the ball up against the backboard. Still, this did not produce many game heroics—that is until I learned how to throw the ball with the perfect velocity at the perfect angle to produce deep fly balls. I could rob the opposition of a potential home run on those. As I ran back, found the wall with my right hand, and leapt high into the air, I would imagine the announcer making the call: *"Back, back, back, he leaps and...MAKES the catch!"*

Except this one time that the announcer's call might have gone more like this: *"Back, back, back, he leaps and... (CRASH) that ball is GONE!"* And then he might have covered his microphone and commented to his broadcast partner, *"And, boy, is that kid in trou-blllle. He's gonna get it when his dad gets home."*

I don't remember my parents making a big deal about their broken window. I do remember being much more careful after that, preferring to pitch and play infield and leave the outfield heroics to another kid on another imaginary diamond. I would eventually play a year of ninth grade basketball, practicing (with permission) while my dad was trying to get some sleep as he was working night shift at the time. I played three very memorable years of high school baseball, as well, with skills honed on a basketball court, of all places.

I came home from college one weekend my freshman year and found most of my family in the backyard. I left my laundry and other belongings in the car and went back to say hello. Dad was jumping on the trampoline with my sisters, and Andy was shooting some hoops on the ol' dirt court. He was trying some long-range buzzer beaters, so I called for the ball to try one from back near the trampoline, probably about 35 feet away.

We counted down, "Threeeee, Twoooo, Ooooone, RRRRRRRRRR!" I released the ball just before the buzzer, and the shot was on line with just about the right distance aaaaannnnddd.... Doink! Off the back iron. Boing! One bounce on the hard dirt. Crash! Right through my parents' bedroom window. I might've been home 15 minutes.

Again, Mom and Dad just accepted the broken window as a mere inconvenience, an inevitable part of having kids who are going to break things. Or perhaps they considered a basketball rim, a few nets, and a couple of replacement windows a small investment for the happiness that we derived from that little dirt basketball court.

37 BOOGER RED

When I was in junior high school, I wanted a motorcycle more than anything on earth. My life would not have been complete without it. I cried myself to sleep many nights because the reality of my riding my own motorcycle seemed so close, yet the reality of my parents' purchasing one seemed light years away. I think that's what hurt so badly back then: I knew they had waaayyy too much sense to trust a kid my age with a motorcycle. But John Earl had one, and Danny had one, and they were younger than I was.

And do you know what my otherwise fiscally responsible (off-the-charts responsible, really) parents did? *They actually bought me a motorcycle!* (This fiscally responsible parent questions—all these years later—why did they go and do a fool thing like that?) Back then, though, I was just about as happy as a mule eatin' briers or a possum eatin' persimmons or any of the other Southern colloquialisms that denote happy beyond happy.

It was a brand-new Honda XL-75. On-off road. 75 cubic centimeters of raw power—it actually would reach about 60 miles per hour down "the quarter," the flat section of road between the store and the Methodist church.

For the most part, I was a responsible driver of my "bike," staying within all the rules of the road (such as they were in Star, Mississippi) and the numerous admonitions of my parents. I was generous with rides back and forth to the store to my brother and sisters. I wanted to prove myself worthy of this most unusual trust that my parents had placed in me.

However, there were a few exceptions that Mom and Dad will probably discover for the first time through the reading of this book. There was this one incident, though, of which they were fully aware.

Booger Red was my uncle's dog, a redbone hound with a deep, soulful—even mournful—howl. And dumb. Man, that dog was dumb. As I like to say, he was D-U-M-M, duuuummmmbbb.

Upon a day, I was riding Andy on my motorcycle, coming back from my grandparents' house. Our usual route was through Pop and Granny's yard, veering left behind Aunt Sissy and Uncle Cecil's house, and then back around to the front of our house. I'll admit we were probably going a little beyond the recommended speed limit as we rounded my aunt and uncle's house—though, in my defense, there was no posted speed limit.

Booger Red was lurking near the back of their house, evidently waiting to pick off any would-be motorcycle traffic. It was the perfect set-up. Speeding motorcycle meets dumb dog. I'm still not sure what that ol' dumb dog thought he was going to accomplish.

I rounded the corner right as Booger Red sprang in front of us. I clipped his rear end, sending him sprawling and sending Andy hurtling off the back of the motorcycle. I somehow managed to keep the motorcycle upright as my older cousin Sonny, who watched the whole incident unfold, ran yelling at me about running over their dog.

I continued on home to report through tears what I had done. Andy was hurt, and the dog was dead, for all I knew. I went ahead and threw the book at myself: I was guilty, though not yet charged, and I was never going to ride that stupid motorcycle again.

My dad sprinted to the scene of the accident to gain a more

accurate assessment of the damage. Andy was a little shaken up by the whole thing but relatively unhurt. Booger Red was fine and dumb as ever. It's hard to hurt a dumb dog. Sonny was probably still mad, but I don't remember Dad saying much about that.

My dad returned home to hand down the strangest punishment I think I have ever had to endure. *He made me get back on the motorcycle and ride. Right then.* Trust me, there was not a much more difficult punishment that he could have conveyed to me that day. But I remounted and rode, per his directive.

I survived to ride (more carefully) another day. There have been many other occasions over the years when I have "wrecked the bike" and had to pick myself back up and ride again. It was a lesson I had learned through a little ol' motorcycle, a dumb ol' dog, and a wise ol' dad.

38 THE TIME WE TOOK MAMA TO RASSLIN'

We called my mom *Mama* until we went away to college and got all sophisticated; then, she became *Mom*. She never really acted very sophisticated, though. After all, she was from out in the country near North Carrollton. She didn't have to go far to get above her raisin'. There was one glaring exception, however. Rasslin' (not to be confused with wrestling—like collegiate or Olympic wrestling) was waaaaayyy below Mama's dignity.

Andy and I watched Mid-South Wrestling every week without fail. We grew up with rasslin' legends like "Cowboy" Bill Watts, Skandar Akbar, the Freebirds, the Rock 'n Roll Express, and Kimala, "the Ugandan Warrior" (who was from Coldwater, Mississippi, as I later discovered). There was Ted DiBiase and Terry "Bam Bam" Gordy, who we used to see occasionally at the Bridges Quickie #3 out on the highway in Star. And Mike Williams, 202 pounds from Mobile, Alabama, everybody's whipping boy who won one match ever (when he was knocked out cold and his tag team partner put him on top of the bad guy for the ol' 1-2-3). And "Captain Redneck" Dick Murdoch, who once did a commercial for Tulsa Welding School that started with his statement, "When I'm not rasslin', I'm weldin'." (Head scratch)

Andy and I had had the opportunity to go to the live rasslin' matches at the Coliseum in Jackson a couple of times. Once, when we were teenagers, our church youth group decided that going to rasslin' would be a fine youth group outing. This is the same youth group that once went to see the movie *Airplane*. That was the movie where the you-know-what hit the fan (literally, it's an *Airplane* thing) with our youth group's sponsors' younger daughters watching. As the adults sat frozen, wondering what they had gotten themselves and all these kids into, D.C. looked over at Ms. Melba and said, "It really hit it, too, didn't it Ms. Melba?!?" (Seat slump, face palm)

I give you to *Airplane* story to show that it wasn't a far stretch for the Wesleyanna UMC youth group to be loading up on a Saturday night to head up to the rasslin' matches. Replete with sponsors. Sponsors that included one Annette Ainsworth, avowed rasslin' snob, whom we had somehow convinced to go with us.

If you've ever been to the live rasslin' matches, you know that people watching is just about as fun as the action inside the "squared circle." People like the grannies who would fight you to the death if you implicated that rasslin' was fake. People like the fan (which, I will remind you, is short for *fanatic*) we saw one time who got so caught up in a come-as-you-are street fight match that he folded up his chair, climbed through the ropes, and joined in the fray himself. Heard that guy got a butt whuppin' back in the security room after the matches were over. This night, Andy and I each kept one eye on the rasslin' matches and one eye on our mama.

I have to say, Mama kept her dignified air throughout the better part of the night. But then, it was time for the main event. I don't remember who the good guy was that night, but he was fighting "The Big Cat" Ernie Ladd in a steel cage match. As is usually the case with a main event, the action started slowly and built throughout the match. Back and forth the grappling went with neither cager gaining a prolonged advantage.

Andy and I were experienced enough rasslin' fans to be familiar with the tempo of a match and how the drama built. (You know, like when one of the rasslers is taking forever to climb to the top corner turnbuckle, and all experienced rasslin' fans know that he's going to get knocked off before he can leap on his theretofore incapacitated opponent.) Well, Mama didn't understand the tempo of the match and, finally, the drama was too much for her. At one point late in the match, the good guy clearly had a big advantage but was taking too much time to make his next move. "The Big Cat" Ernie Ladd, meanwhile—and unbeknownst to the good guy though thousands were trying to inform him—was staggering to his feet. My rasslin' proper mama finally could take it no longer. She bounced to her feet and hollered, "Hit him!!! Hit him!!!"

My mama, who had only agreed to accompany us on this mind-numbing adventure as a chaperone, had clearly and unequivocally engaged in what she had heretofore called "pure stupidity." There she was, yelling with all her might with all the other minions at "The Big Cat" Ernie Ladd. In front of God and everybody. It was a church outing, after all.

I don't think Mom has watched a rasslin match, even on TV, ever since. She denies my recollection of the events of that night, but my brother attests to the validity of my account, for what that's worth. Either way, the time we took Mama to rasslin' will forever be a part of our family's lore.

39 UP (TO MY WAIST IN) THE CREEK

Until the last couple of years, one of the highlights of our family Christmas gathering at my parents' house had been the annual tractor ride. Dad would hitch a trailer to the back of his tractor and take us all the way to the back side of Uncle Hob's place. We would go through the woods, up and down steep hills, and through creeks. We were constantly dodging branches, bracing ourselves for bumps along the way, and generally just enjoying being on the annual tractor ride.

The family tractor ride began when my nephews Daniel and Ryne were small. Over the years as grandchildren were added and as they grew, the trailer became more and more crowded, but we always made room for everyone. There was one part of the ride in which I steadfastly refused to participate, however. After crossing through the creek (and trying to avoid being splashed) and weaving among a number of lofty trees, we would make a sharp turn to the right and down a hill to a pair of steel rails that spanned the creek. As Dad slowed to make sure the tractor tires were squarely on the rails, I would always slip off the back of the trailer and follow on foot until it was safely up the other side.

One reason I always stepped off was the one time when the trailer tires slipped off the rails. The trailer bottomed out—still on the rails—and Dad dragged us on across the rails until the trailer tires found firm ground. Aside from a few compromised tailbones, everyone was okay. I think my aversion to crossing the creek on the steel bridge goes back much further than the annual tractor rides.

As a young teenager, I was squirrel hunting one day with Uncle Cecil in that part of the woods. It was a very cold morning, and we had not even taken a shot at a squirrel. We were moving from one part of the woods to another, probably toward the enormous oak tree that we had labeled the Squirrel Hotel because of its many nests. Uncle Cecil came to a good place to jump the creek and half-jumped, half-stepped across. I followed suit, but about halfway through my half-jump, half-step, I realized I should have included a little more jump and a little less step. Into the creek I went. Though I kept my shotgun safely above the water, I was soaked from the waist down. Uncle Cecil spun around and faced me with a how-in-the-world-did-you-manage-to-do-that look on his face. I met his incredulous gaze with an I'm-cold-and-wet-and-ready-to-go-home look of my own.

Not too long after the squirrel hunting incident, I fell in the creek again. I was riding motorcycles with my friends Danny and Ronnie on the terrace rows behind Pop and Granny's house. We became bored with jumping the hills and decided to ride down one of the many trails through the woods. Not far into our ride, we encountered a steel I-beam rail across the creek. Danny and Ronnie crossed first, and I was close behind. As I was crossing, though, my front tire hit a piece of metal that was sticking out from the edge of the rail. You guessed it – down I went into the creek with my motorcycle tumbling after me. By the grace of God, one of my little side mirrors caught on the steel beam and held the motorcycle dangling in the air until the three of us could pull it back up. Me, well, I was in the all-too-familiar position of soaked from the waist down but otherwise unharmed.

A couple of years ago, our extended family Christmas time moved to our house, and everyone seems happy enough with the venue change except for the loss of the annual tractor ride. That is bemoaned every year, especially by the grandkids. I miss it, too, but through all the years of tractor rides, I feel like I somehow escaped another inevitable plunge into the creek. Best not to push it.

40 RUNNING FROM A WHOOPIN'

Note: If you never took a whoopin' as a child, just know that you probably deserved plenty of them. Heck, you might need one right now. If that applies to you or if you're one of those people who don't believe parents should ever whoop their young 'uns, feel free to just skip this chapter; you'll probably just get mad anyway.

I earned myself plenty of whoopin's as a kid. Unlike the present generation, we understood whoopin's to be a regular part of life then. My sisters and brother and I understood that if we misbehaved, we had made a down payment on a whoopin'. Well, Andy was a little slow on the learning curve when it came to behaving in church, but that's a whole 'nother story.

If we were seen around town with thin red stripes on our legs, everyone would have understood that we (not our parents) likely did something outside the realm of acceptable behavior. They would have understood that we had been instructed to go pick our own switch and that we had been subsequently whooped with said switch. (By the way, if you've never had to pick your own switch, it's a no-win situation. The small, thin ones have this whip-like action that stings. The bigger ones, well that's like getting hit with a tree branch. Okay, that's a stretch, perhaps, but it was a Catch-22 to pick your own switch, to be sure.)

Let me be clear that there was never any question before, during, or after any of these whoopin's that we even questioned—much less, doubted—our parents' love for us. Though our family didn't say "I love you" very much, and we weren't especially big on hugs then, either, whether or not we were loved was simply not an issue. It was just the way things were back then, and it made us tougher. We would need that toughness when we had to endure the rigors of walking to school in the snow, uphill both ways with nothing but a biscuit in our lunch pail. (To my now-appalled friends from the North, I am waxing a bit hyperbolic. Our *parents and grandparents* were the ones who did the whole walking to school in the snow with one biscuit bit....)

There was this one time around my early teenage years when I did something deserving of a whoopin' and simply decided that I was not taking one that day. I don't remember what it was that I did, but I remember me well enough to know that I probably deserved the aforementioned whoopin'. Nevertheless, quite imprudently, I made some smart-aleck remark and fled from my mama and the belt that served as her whoopin' administrator of choice that day.

Down the hall and into my sisters' room I ran. I slammed the door behind myself and locked it. Their two windows were about head-high, but I had climbed onto the bed and was quickly devising an escape plan when I heard the screwdriver in the door. Wow, that was quicker than I had expected! The click of the lock giving way came seconds later and before I could remove the screen and climb through the window.

I took two whoopin's that day, one from Mom when she successfully navigated the labyrinth that I had forced upon her and another from Dad when he got home from work that day. I am fairly certain that I deserved the first spanking, but I know beyond a shadow of a doubt that I deserved the second one. Because any good Southern boy can tell you that about the worst crime against humanity that you can commit is to sass yo mama.

41 HIS VERSUS HERS

One of the most entertaining arguments in the Ainsworth home throughout my teenage years was the Dad's holidays versus Mom's holidays debate. It was a good-natured quarrel, rooted in the fact that by then, they both had solid jobs with good benefits. Dad was a trailer mechanic with Yellow Freight, and Mom was a rural letter carrier for the United States Postal Service.

In all fairness one received about the same number of paid holidays as the other. Outside of the big six, though, their holidays did not often line up with one another. The argument would start something like this:

Mom (with a competitive grin): "I'm off work tomorrow!"

Anyone else in the family: "Why, what's tomorrow?"

Mom: "Columbus Day."

Someone else, usually me: "Really? Columbus Day? So, which one of the many Columbus Day celebrations will you be attending this year?"

Mom: "Well, what about the days your daddy gets off work?"

And then it was on. Back and forth it would go. Veteran's Day (Mom). Anniversary with the company (Dad). President's Day

(Mom). Birthday (Dad). The birthday holiday was a particular special one to Dad since he was born on New Year's Day; that meant two consecutive days off for him or overtime pay if he chose to work either day.

The four of us kids always sided with Dad, probably because Mom usually started the friendly squabble—remember, we had a heightened sense of fairness. Mom's case against Dad's holidays being more "out there" was certainly legitimate, however. We would accuse Mom of getting Valentine's Day off, inquire as to the date of Earth Day that year, wonder how she planned to celebrate Arbor Day.

Our coup de gras was Groundhog Day. Like many of the others that we included on her holiday list, she didn't actually receive Groundhog Day as a holiday, of course. Even after I went away to college, I tried to remember to call her every February 2 and ask if she had enjoyed her holiday. When I would forget to call, she would often call to remind me. This went on until she retired from the postal service. Funny how a playful argument can turn into a connecting point.

My parents have both long since retired now. Several years ago, I was attending a conference in Jackson, so I called them to see if they could meet me for lunch near the conference site. I love my Dad's response: "Shoot, we're retired. We can do what we want."

Indeed. Whether or not it's Groundhog Day.

42 I ONLY CHEATED ONCE

My family carries a number of distinguishable traits. We are ultra-competitive, we have a magnified sense of fairness, we are very literal in our humor to the point of annoyance, and we are rule followers. My sisters and brother and I were instilled with a code of ethics that has served us well. As a result, my foray into the criminal world was brief and consequential.

The only item I ever stole was when I was a little fella of about six or seven. The object of my sticky fingers was a two-cent piece of grape bubble gum from a candy rack near one of the registers at Howard Brothers in Pearl. While Mom and the checkout clerk were busy with Mom's items, I felt an irrepressible desire for a piece of grape bubble gum. I slipped it into my pocket undetected and walked to the car, amazed that I had been able to pull off a crime of this magnitude.

Later, in private, I slipped the gum out of its wrapper and anticipated an even greater satisfaction than usual because of the primeval method in which I had procured it. The sugary grapen goodness lasted no longer than a usual piece of Super Bubble, however, and then the guilt set in. I had committed the perfect crime because no one knew. I found that I was also left to carry the remorse alone. About ten or fifteen years later, Howard Brothers went out of business. I never read or heard the reason why, but deep down I knew that a bunch of little boys had surely stolen enough grape Super Bubble over the years to put them under. I just knew it. And I never stole another thing (unless, of course, you count my swiping of my dad's cigarettes when I was in seventh grade).

I also only cheated once. I didn't have much need to cheat as I made good grades throughout my school years, finishing as valedictorian of my senior class. Education was very important in our family; Lu Ann, Wilagene, Andy, and I never doubted we would attend college because of the priority of education my parents instilled in us. Mom and Dad had both gone beyond the normal high school education. Mom had gone to Holmes Junior College and Dad—well, he had that extra year of high school. So we worked hard in school and competed intensely and fairly.

Until the day in my first period biology class when a conversation with a classmate revealed a forgotten algebra assignment due the next period. I panicked and "borrowed" said classmate's homework and busily scribbled down as much as I could before class started. Ms. Mengelson walked over unannounced (the unmitigated gall!) and noticed my frantic scribbling. Turns out, she and Ms. Brown had this agreement that if either caught anyone copying homework for their classes, they would rat the students out to the other. (Shouldn't that necessarily be a stated policy at the beginning of the year for the sake of would-be cheaters?)

Ms. Brown doled out the expected punishment, a zero on the assignment. That was okay; I understood. But it wasn't as if I couldn't **do** the work I had copied; I just didn't have **time**. I was an ace at algebra, having already used it to calculate that I could still make my usual *A* for the term. However, Ms. Brown had what was, for me, a much more potent consequence: an automatic *F* on that term's citizenship grade. Oh no! I would not be able to keep this from my parents.

Guilt ate at me for the rest of the term. How would I tell my parents that I had cheated and brought utter disgrace to the family? Somewhere near report card day, I noticed a fortuitous coincidence that might ultimately work in my favor. Our school basketball team played an away game on the day report cards were to be sent home! I would not see any playing time in that game but no matter; it would gain me several hours' stay before I delivered the report card of shame.

Maybe my parents would be so ready for bed when I arrived home that they would just sign the bright orange cards and be done with it. Maybe they would allow me to summarize my otherwise stellar grades as they just routinely signed them. Yes, maybe they wouldn't even notice....

No such luck. They noticed; I explained. Confession brought healing and the requisite signatures. Mom and Dad seemed content with my summation that I had learned my lesson and would never let it happen again. We went to bed, and I never cheated again.

43 LESSONS FROM POP

Pop was on into his 60's when I was born, so he always seemed old to me. He was retired from a career in the railroad, so the only work I ever knew him to do was around the house. Pop mowed around the house with a push mower while Granny mowed the wider expanses with their riding mower. They also had a garden that they both worked throughout the spring and summer months.

I remember another time when Pop, Dad, and Uncle Hob cut down a giant red oak in the woods near Pop's house. Now, a red oak is the easiest tree to cut and to split into firewood, but this tree was massive, the biggest that I had ever seen taken to the ground. Chain saws, axes, mauls, and wedges were all required to cut and split the wood. I remember watching my dad and my uncle working away on this enormous tree with my grandfather, wondering how many times in the past they had worked together in such a manner but with more primitive equipment. I also remember being impressed that Pop could still tackle a project as big as that red oak at his age.

I remember Pop purposely taking on the role of teacher in my life on two different occasions. The first set of lessons with Pop came after my parents bought me my first baseball glove, a red Revelation from Western Auto. Pop fished out his old glove from who knows where to play catch with me. His glove was one of those old, pancake-flat gloves with the enormous padded fingers. There was no pocket in which the ball would naturally settle, so he always had to use two hands while catching the ball. That was a good model for a kid just learning to catch a baseball.

I don't remember how many times we played catch, but I recall Pop giving me several pointers: two hands while catching, step where you're going to throw—simple instructions like that. More than the coaching points, I just recollect that he got out there in his front yard with that old puffy mitt of his and threw the ball back and forth with his grandson. In the years since Pop's death in the late '80's, I have searched for that old mitt of his several times with no luck. He must have thrown it away at some point, not knowing how much it would mean in the future to either of his grandsons who would develop a lifelong love for baseball, two grandsons who would eventually go on to coach high school baseball.

Driving lessons with Pop would come about ten years later, and one particular lesson comes up about as often as my family reconvenes to dredge up the stories of the past. Pop's car was a baby blue Capri whose span covered about a quarter of an acre—or so it seemed. His car was not only spacious, but it also had a three-speed manual transmission. Yikes! The simulators in my driver education class didn't have clutches. I guess Pop had determined that if I could drive his car, then I could drive any car. He was right...eventually. Our initial drive, however, was a memorable adventure.

After some difficulty between first and second gear that required a stop to unstick the gears, we were on our way. I drove out of their circular gravel driveway, onto the road in front of the house, and eventually onto what we called "the big road." I had to go through the gears a couple of times, getting the hang of that, but I was now driving toward town and the greater potential of other vehicles complicating our lesson. I suppose Pop figured I had learned enough for one day. As we crossed the railroad track and were approaching the Star Volunteer Fire Department on the right, Pop said, "Turn around right up here."

Now, what Pop *meant* was for me to turn around at the spacious intersection just past the fire department. (It was not a big deal to turn around in the middle of an intersection, as there was very little traffic at any time in Star.) What I *heard*—literalist that I am—was to turn around just past the driveway of the fire department where there was a little shoulder to start my turn. So...after checking both directions for any approaching vehicles, I began my large, sweeping turn. Now, I had not yet come to the point in my driver education where I could accurately predict the correct circumference of a U-turn, especially when driving a tank. And so...I ran over the hedges opposite the fire department. Ran slap over them. Not just one bush but the better part of a whole row of boxwoods. They popped back into place but not before quite the beatdown.

When the family stories are told and re-told, the question still comes up, "Do you remember the time you ran over the hedges?" Yes. Yes, I do. As if my family would ever let me forget. In fairness to Pop's memory, though, he never said a word. He let me tell on myself.

44 ABERCROMBIE JUMPS ON THE GRILL

My sisters were terrible at naming animals. They named a cat Kiki—because, you know, cats come when you call, "Ki ki ki ki." We had a dog named Jobo, a name Andy and I lengthened to Joseph Beauregard. That was the dog Lu Ann taught to growl and attack us every time my brother or I approached my sisters' room. *Jobo* was not a bad name itself; however, while we had Jobo, we took in a cat that they named. . . Bo. Oh, **that** was creative. As usual, my brother and I took upon ourselves the responsibility of renaming the cat to something with a little more flair.

We settled on *Abercrombie*. No, not after the clothing company; that didn't exist then, as far as I know. Abercrombie's namesake was Pittsburgh Steelers' running back Walter Abercrombie. The cat didn't remind us of Walter Abercrombie in the least; Andy and I just liked his unusual surname. So *Bo* became *Abercrombie*, even if just to my brother and me.

Abercrombie provided the most indistinguishable moment between real life and cartoon life that I have ever experienced. The setting was on our back porch on a Friday night. I know it was a Friday night because Mom was grilling hamburgers, and we ate hamburgers almost every Friday night of my growing-up years. Dad, Andy, Wilagene, and I were sitting outside talking while Mom was putting the hamburgers on the grill. The grill was located near the edge of the concrete so that the grease drippings that weren't caught by the drip can would fall on the ground. All of our animals—dogs and cats alike—were scavengers who eagerly awaited the grease drippings. On this particular Friday night, Abercrombie was first in line.

Maybe he thought he would get bumped in line later by one of the dogs. Maybe he had a heightened sense of adventure on this particular night. Maybe he just wasn't thinking because he was a dumb cat (and, yes, I do realize that *dumb cat* is a redundant term). Regardless of the reason, as the pleasant aroma of grilling burgers began to permeate our immediate area, Abercrombie's curiosity was aroused. The time came for Mom to flip the burgers, and when she raised the top to the grill, the pleasant Friday night aroma exploded into a pungent combination of sizzle, smoke, and smell of perfectly seasoned beef. This was more than Abercrombie could stand, so much so that all of us took notice. All of us, that is, except Mom—and she was the only one who could have stopped what happened next.

As Mom flipped the last burger, she closed the grill and turned away, Abercrombie seized his opportunity to skip from sumptuous grease drippings to their source. He glanced left, quickly scanned back to the right, and leapt. I'm not sure what he expected at the apex of his jump, perhaps a table set for curious cats who skip steps to secure culinary shortcuts, but what he landed on was a grill lid that was hotter than his little paws were prepared to handle.

The following moment—though it spanned maybe three seconds—was a collision of real life with super slow motion. The reality of the scorching grill did not strike Abercrombie until he had stood still for a full second, and then the scene that I had seen many times in various Saturday morning cartoons came alive on our back patio on that Friday night. Four paws went four directions with Abercrombie's tail extended due south. Hair all over his terrified body stood straight up as he pronounced his panic from this startling turn of events.

And just like that, the scene was over. Mom turned around to see what this ruckus was behind her, a ruckus that had Andy, Dad, Wilagene, and I doubled over, clutching our sides. To Mom, it was a quick little commotion; to us, it was a moment that has now been frozen for over 30 years, an unexpected comic relief on an otherwise humdrum hamburger Friday night.

45 DON'T EVER SAY YOU'VE NEVER

I remember one time in 10th grade telling a friend that I had never broken a bone or gotten stitches. Don't ever say you've never broken a bone. It's bad luck. I don't really even believe in luck— good or bad—or karma or anything like that, but the timing of my comment proved awfully suspicious.

During the middle of the fall of my sophomore year, I broke my ankle at football practice. The team suffered greatly for it, let me tell you. That one game late in the season when we were down about 60 to Puckett—I might have entered the game a play or two in that one. The broken ankle proved to be the end of my less-than-promising football career. Oh, the ankle injury wasn't horrific or anything like that. Having never played football before that year, though, I had significantly underestimated the force that one body lined with armor can generate against another.

In the modern world of sports, I would have simply chosen to "focus on baseball." However, there was no such go-to cop-out phrase in the fall of '81, when openness and honesty prevailed. No, I had to man up and talk with Coach Brister face to face and tell him that...Mom didn't want me to play football anymore. Which, I suppose, was *technically* true. And we Ainsworths, we're literalists, after all.

Coach Brister could have used that conversation to try to

shame me into staying on the team, and he probably could have been successful, too (though as a keen judge of talent, I'm sure he saw the futility for both of us in my continued role as a football player). Instead, he offered me a chance to be a part of the team without the repeated collisions to which I had become so averse. If I do say so myself, Coach Brister got himself a stomp-down (*Abboism alert!*) good football manager for the next two years. I received an education in statistics, sports medicine, management, and equipment repair that would serve me well in a future career as a high school coach. (And I got in all the games for free....)

I had sufficiently recovered from my broken ankle by the following spring to play the sport I had truly loved since childhood. The 1981-82 school year was McLaurin High School's first as a high school. As a result, our baseball field had yet to be built when the time rolled around for baseball season. Baseball practice took place on the football field that year, a notion that would have made the skin of every football coach I've ever known crawl. Nevertheless, this is where my second incident of the year took place.

I was the team's first baseman, and all of the infielders were taking ground balls that day. We had been ingrained with the discipline of fielding ground balls with two hands. The football field was not as level as it might have appeared from a distance, and one of the many bad hops that the field produced found my bare right hand and ricocheted into the outfield. Disappointed that I hadn't made the play, I dropped my head to discover my hand covered with blood.

Coach Butts sent me immediately to the school office for medical assistance. I had a little fun at the office ladies' expense by walking in with my blood-streaked hand held in front of me and asking if I could get a Band-Aid. A trip to the doctor's office revealed a cracked bone at the tip of my ring finger in addition to the separated fingernail. Wear this brace, the doctor instructed, and try to keep from using the finger for a few days. I was back at baseball practice the following day, deftly fielding grounders with one hand held behind my back.

My third incident within about eight months of making the ill-fated statement about the soundness of my body happened that summer. I had warned my brother repeatedly to keep his stinkin' hands off my baseball gloves, but the learning curve was a little steep for him. He is left-handed, anyway, so I still don't understand the fascination with sneaking my gloves, but it was a recurring problem with us. On the day Greg Bordeaux came over to throw baseball with me, the issue came to a head. As Bordeaux's car passed the front window, I began to walk up the stairs out of our den...just in time to see Andy sneaking up the hall with my glove...again.

The race was on to the back door, a race he won. He flung the wooden door backward as I was reaching for it. CRASH! The glass pane in the door shattered as it met my hand. I could feel shards of glass imbedded in my arm, including one that had stuck in my wrist, causing no small amount of blood loss. Off to the emergency room we went. This time, I needed nine stitches on my wrist and four more on a wound we discovered further up the same forearm after arriving at the hospital.

The nurses gave me plenty of time to gather myself before we prepared to leave. When I finally felt stable enough to walk without assistance, my parents and I walked to the desk just outside the examination room. They signed all the pertinent forms, and we should have been able to leave. One of the nurses, however, alerted another nurse to bring her a wheelchair as she moved quickly toward me.

"I'm okay, really," I assured her.

"Not for you," she responded, "for her."

My poor mama. She had handled the whole incident so well, making sure that I had kept pressure on the wound and keeping me conscious with the aid of a well-timed ammonia cap. And on Dad's and her anniversary, too. Now that I was all fixed up, the time had come for her to swoon. Another 10 minutes for Mom's sake, and we were on our way.

Andy was fearfully waiting at home. Having had a few hours to work on his heartfelt delivery of the requisite apology, he delivered it with great sincerity. I had lost too much blood to have the strength to give him the beatdown that he deserved, so I just accepted it.

After those eight months of intermittent pain, I cringe whenever I hear anyone claim they have never broken a bone or needed stitches. My ankle pops, and my fingertip swells, and my wrist gets a little painful to the touch.

"Let me tell you about the time I said that..." I begin.

46 STATUS SYMBOL OF CHOICE

For the better part of 10 years of school, most of the shirts I wore had a number on them. The ones that didn't were mostly generic team shirts from my favorite teams from all sports. I couldn't have cared less about fashion trends. Somewhere in my 10th grade year, though, that began to change. I'm sure my burgeoning attraction to the opposite sex had everything to do with my fashion epiphany.

For many in my generation (Class of '84-ish), the clothing status symbol of choice was the Izod shirt. The Polo had not yet gathered enough momentum—at least in Star, Mississippi—to supplant it yet. I eventually owned a light brown Izod, but I must confess that the shirt was secondary to a much greater clothing status symbol at my school, one that I had earlier longed to attain: Levi jeans with a circle imprint on one of the rear pockets.

I longed to be one of the "in" crowd with the circle-pocket jeans. These jeans couldn't simply be bought; they were more of a process. The easy part was to buy a pair of boot cut Levi's. The ring itself required months of carrying a can of Skoal (or Copenhagen for those who could go hard core). This was a problem for me, as I did not dip snuff. Sure, I could have carried a can just to get its imprint; however, a poser would have certainly been exposed, and I had my pride.

One day on a whim, I decided to cross over into coolness. I was hanging out with my friend Greg Bordeaux when he finished one can of Skoal and stopped by the store for another. He knew my predicament (except for the jeans envy part) and offered to let me take a pinch of his tobacco to see if I liked it. Well, that was polite on his part and certainly intuitive, but I reasoned that the sooner I started carrying my own can, the sooner I would have my own imprinted jeans.

Bordeaux and I were standing in front of my dad's shop when I opened my brand new can of Skoal. Because it was a new can, I could not yet learn that nifty shaking-the-can thing that dippers do to pack all the tobacco tightly against the edge of the can. Bordeaux, now firmly entrenched as my dipping mentor, could teach me that later. Now, it was time for me to go all in.

I reached into the can to get a fairly sizable pinch of snuff. Bordeaux cautioned me that I might want to start a little smaller. I had previously experimented with chewing tobacco, and I didn't see the difference between the two except packaging, cut, and the obvious cool factor. You can see where this was going....

For a few moments, I was able to bask in the glow of my newly established "habit" and dream of my full range of jeans and their future ring imprints. Then, the world began to shift, ever so slightly at first, then more rapidly as the seconds lengthened into minutes. I excused myself and moved quickly toward the house before the earth could give way underneath me.

This would be a good time in the story to tell you just how much I have always hated throwing up. I knew I was on the verge of vomiting on this day, and the thought was about as dreadful to me as the tsunami churning in my stomach. I sat on the couch with my head in my hands between my knees for about a solid hour before I dared stand up or even open my eyes again. The nausea finally passed and with it, my desire for circle-pocket jeans.

Bordeaux went home that day with a practically full can of Skoal in *each* back pocket of his Levis. I, on the other hand, would go on to buy a light brown shirt with a tiny alligator on the chest and form a mild addiction to Jolly Ranchers and sunflower seeds.

47 A NEAR TRAGEDY

When I was in high school, football Fridays were days of routine. I was the manager for the McLaurin Tiger football team, a position that both helped me avoid the pain of football to which I seemed allergic and prepared me for a future coaching career. Fridays were the same each week that we hosted a game. It was this routine that led to a near tragedy.

After school, which would always include a pep rally at the end of every football Friday, I had a list of responsibilities that would carry me and our other managers all the way until game time at Tiger Stadium. I would get a few dollars from Coach Rogers and drive down the road to Thomasville Grocery to buy him a pack of H.B. Scott and five pieces of bubble gum along with a pocketful of Jolly Ranchers for me. By the end of the game, Coach Rogers would have that entire pack of chewing tobacco and all five pieces of gum in his mouth, quite a sight to behold.

The rest of the afternoon was spent repairing equipment, preparing stat sheets, and taping ankles. Somewhere in all the activity, the managers would join the team for a pre-game meal in the cafeteria. Finally, the time came for the special teams units to take the field for pre-game warm-ups, followed soon after by the rest of the team. One quick trip back across the school driveway to the fieldhouse for a few inspirational words later, and game time would arrive.

For the managers, duties were assigned, and each person moved toward his assigned role. My Friday night role was keeping statistics and making sure all other managerial tasks were being fulfilled. I would give our coaches a quick statistical update during halftime, and then it was back to the field for the second half. After the game, I called in the score and vital statistics to the newspaper and cleaned up the training room before leaving for home.

My high school, which looks much the same today as it did some 30 years ago, has a unique layout that plays a key role in this story. From two-lane Star Road, the school sits a couple hundred yards back. The driveway leading to the school can best be described as a large, rounded rectangle, and it encircles (*enrectangles*?) the football field. The west side of the field is the visitor's side, and this was where the buses exited school every day.

The east side of the school driveway dissected the football field and the fieldhouse. Between the home bleachers and the driveway was a gravel strip where most of the football players, coaches, and managers parked. The rest of the students and the majority of the Friday night football crowd parked near the school. Usually, by the time I had finished my managerial duties and driven out the east drive, the parking lot was a ghost town.

One late fall night, toward the end of football season, the public address announcer gave instructions that all vehicles were to exit from the west drive, essentially making the driveway a one-way street. However, much to my later dismay, this announcement was made during halftime when I was in the fieldhouse along with the rest of the team. I'm not sure if these instructions were later given to the football team; once again, I had duties after the game that would have precluded me from hearing them then, as well.

I finished up a little early that night because I was to be leaving later the same night on a Boy Scout camping trip. I crossed the driveway with my brother to where my car was parked in its usual place in the gravel strip. I exited out the *east* drive in my usual manner.

I noticed as I turned on the road in front of the school that the parking lot hadn't completely emptied yet. This was a little different from my normal routine, but I was careful to make sure that the car at the front of the west exit wasn't going to pull out suddenly when WHAM!!! Out of nowhere a resounding thud just below my window shattered my concentration. Before I could get my head around what had just happened, I saw blue lights coming up fast behind me. I pulled over and the officer proceeded to lambast me for trying to run him over. Andy and I were both in a fearful state of shock.

As the deputy was going through a laundry list of what he was going to do to me and what he wanted to do on top of that, I was able to reconstruct what had just happened. The officer, dressed in all dark brown and without a reflective vest, had been directing traffic with his flashlight. I had never seen him as his back was turned away from me; furthermore, my concentration had been on the traffic exiting from that end of the driveway. He would naturally have assumed that I had heard the announcement about the traffic flow and addressed me from this assumption.

When the deputy explicitly said that he had swung his flashlight to hit me in the head, I realized that a lonely stretch of road was *not* where I needed to be with this officer with his current temperament. Grateful already that Andy was with me, I began to beg the officer to take me back to the school to call my dad, repeatedly apologizing and telling him that I hadn't seen him. He obviously did not believe this but ultimately relented, allowing me to drive back to the fieldhouse while he followed closely behind me.

Andy and I walked into the fieldhouse, visibly shaken, with the officer angrily following closely behind. My principal, Mr. Harlan Stanley, was there talking with the football coaches. He could tell immediately that something was wrong. A large, imposing figure,

Mr. Stanley began to move toward us.

"Mr. Stanley, do you know this boy?" the officer demanded.

"Yes, sir, I sure do. He's one of the finest young men at our school."

I will never, ever forget Mr. Stanley's words or the finality with which he spoke them. The conversation that had been so one-sided just down the road took a much different tone when my principal started this one with the assumption that if I said I hadn't seen the officer, then I really hadn't seen him. I don't remember much of the rest of the exchange from that point. I just knew that Mr. Stanley was on my side of this whole mess and that it would end favorably for me.

The deputy was quickly ushered from the fieldhouse, and I was on my way home and then to a late night campout. The deputies all over the county were wearing reflective vests within a week or two after the incident. I still wince at the memory of that flashlight hammering my car and the fact that my head was the intended target. I take no joy, however, in the fact that the deputy who swung it was killed a year or two later by prisoners he was transporting.

Sometimes, you have a moment of clarity in life when all your home training comes home to roost. When Mr. Harlan Stanley—before he knew any details of the incident—staked his reputation as the leader of our school on 15 words spoken firmly on my behalf, it was one of those moments of clarity. I was immediately grateful for everything that my parents had ever taught me about honesty and integrity and hard work and respect for authority. Traits learned over many years came home to roost in that moment when I realized that Mr. Stanley had my back.

48 BUILDING A BASEBALL PROGRAM FROM THE GROUND UP

I have a box full of academic medals and certificates from my high school days in my attic somewhere. In that box are my honor cords from graduation, several subject area awards, and something that says I was valedictorian of my senior class. I was voted Mr. McLaurin and Most Likely to Succeed by my fellow students. I feel blessed to have been so honored, and I am grateful for all of the opportunities my academic standing afforded me. However, the accomplishment from my high school days of which I am most proud is being a part of building a high school baseball program from the ground up.

On my best days in the classroom, I was an *A* student with the potential to excel far beyond high school. Though I had several teachers who pushed me, that part of high school came easily enough to me. On my best days on the baseball field, I attained mediocrity with no potential to play beyond high school. (In case you read false humility into that last sentence, I can put you in touch with many former teammates who can verify the veracity of my valuation of my abilities on the diamond.) Baseball, though, had been my first love, and I had fallen hard.

The recreational league in Star only offered playing opportunities through age 12, and I thought my career had stalled at that point. When word came that before my sophomore year, Florence High School would split into three schools—Florence, Richland, and McLaurin High Schools—my interest was piqued. Further, juniors and seniors would be able to finish at Florence even if they lived in another district. I began to do the math for my high school baseball opportunities. The math became simple when tryouts drew an underwhelming number of hopefuls, and just like that, I was on the team.

I remember where I was when I learned that I would be a starter on the baseball team. As I was taking care of business in the bathroom by the gym, Coach Butts came in and stood at the urinal next to me.

"Ainsworth," he said without making eye contact (because that would have been weird), "You ever played first base?"

"A few times," I replied. I couldn't let on that first base would not have been my position of choice, nor was it one at which I had had much experience. I had learned long before that you always said yes to an opportunity to play, no matter the position.

"Well, you're going to be my first baseman. You're the tallest kid on the team."

Okay, so I didn't win the position because I was necessarily skilled for it, but on opening day, there I stood as the starting first baseman for a high school baseball team. All six feet, 135 pounds of me. I was surrounded mostly by freshmen and eighth graders and Curtis Potter, the junior standout athlete who could have excelled at Florence but who had made the decision to come to our school and help us build an athletic program.

It didn't matter that we didn't have a field and had to play all our games on the road that year. It didn't matter that we only (mercifully) played 10 games that year. It didn't matter that we didn't win any of them. It didn't even matter...eventually...that I made a bad throw that cost us the only close game we played that year against Bentonia and their skinny little pitcher, Roderick

Barnes, who would go on to become the head basketball coach at Ole Miss. It didn't matter that year because my teammates and I were high school baseball players.

I have quite a few memories from that 0-10 season in 1982. Practicing on the football field. The ground ball in practice that cracked a bone at the end of my right ring finger, which I'm still reminded of when I clip the mis-shaped fingernail on that finger. The time Billy Joe Walker tracked a fly ball, calling "I got it! I got it! I got it!" and then getting doinked on the head by it. The time Marcus Riley neglected to tie his sweat pants during headfirst sliding drills in the mud, right by the driveway where all the buses were lined up. Yep, catcalls aplenty for that full moon in broad daylight.

Somewhere between my sophomore and junior years, someone convinced our baseball team that we had the potential to be good. Like, make-the-playoffs good. We were a year older, a little bigger, and a little stronger. We had our own field to practice and play on by then. Oh, and no small factor: we were dropping down to the lowest classification of schools.

Though we struggled through our non-district schedule, we would finish my junior season 9-1 in our district. We clinched the district championship on the road on the afternoon of high school graduation. We arrived back at the gym just in time for Curtis and our other seniors to don gowns over their baseball uniforms and replace baseball caps with graduation caps. The rest of the team, still in full uniform, stayed to cheer them on.

I would be remiss in relating my childhood stories, my baseball memories in particular, to neglect the one loss our team suffered in district play that year. It wasn't so much that we lost to Piney Woods, the worst team on our schedule. Piney Woods brought hope to those on our team who were slow afoot, like me. *Everyone* could steal against Piney Woods. I reached first base early in the game and, sure enough, Coach Butts gave me the steal sign. I looked down as I measured my lead, ready to go at the pitcher's first motion. My mistake was in looking down. When I raised my eyes, the ball was already in flight toward to first base. Picked off against Piney Woods! My dad and brother will never let me forget it. I shared the story with every team I ever coached after that so that none of my players would make my mistake or suffer the embarrassment of it.

During my high school days, baseball playoffs took the form of four-team tournaments. The winners and runners-up from the North State and South State tournaments, hosted by one of the teams in each tournament, would meet at a neutral site to decide the state title in another double-elimination tournament. We had the advantage of hosting the Class B (equivalent of today's Class A) South State tournament. That advantage quickly turned sour, however. We were promptly bounced from the tournament by first-day losses to Hickory and Beaumont (in their hideous bright gold and blue softball-looking uniforms). Rain set in for the next few days, and my teammates and I worked out our disappointment by working the muddy field so that the remaining participants could play for our longed-for tickets to the state tournament.

We entered my senior season with the state Class BB playoffs as our goal. We had moved back up in classification to BB (now AA) and into one of the toughest districts in the state. Not only were the defending district champions back and still strong, we had moved up from Class B and the champions of the area's Class A (now AAA) district had moved down, all into a crowded competition for one playoff spot.

Our core group had experienced an irresistible taste of playoff baseball. Though our stay was brief, it served as fuel for the 1984 season, my senior season. No longer content to just put on the forest green and old gold McLaurin uniforms, we were hungrier than ever and worked hard all during the off-season to continue to climb the ladder of success.

Danny "Dawg" Knight, just a pup in 1982, had become a force

behind the plate two years later. He was such a fiery competitor that he once blocked an errant pitch that cracked his, er, private protective gear and stayed in the game. Jeff Walker and Sidney "Sid-no" Wheatley alternated between shortstop and pitcher, giving us consistency in those two spots. Tim "Hise" Nicely had gone from the shy kid who always looked down and toed the dirt when Coach Butts corrected him to a key bat in the middle of our line-up. Tim endured an arm injury that year that necessitated a move across the diamond to my usual first base spot. I moved briefly to third and then settled into the designated hitter/first base coach/batting practice pitcher role. I usually hit for our only other senior that year, speedy right fielder Dennis "Flip" Wilson.

Mike Byrd and Mike "Deadeye" Abel were newcomers who would help catapult us to another level. Vernon "Sick Chicken" Mangum, the only player of the team slower than me (on a given day) offered the ability to play multiple positions and was well known among his teammates for his unbelievable self-calculated on-base percentage. I had even packed on 20 pounds of muscle onto my lean frame by the spring of 1984, though not one pound of it ever helped me hit a curve ball. And as always, our fiery field general, Coach Charlie Butts, put us through the paces as ballplayers and as young men learning about life.

McLaurin baseball was a family affair for the Ainsworths. My brother Andy was the manager of that team, and my sister Lu Ann was one of our scorekeepers. My parents came to every game that Dad's work schedule allowed, and Wilagene may have even made a game or two.

We played a tough non-district schedule in preparation for a playoff run and were able to notch some wins over much larger teams, including next-town rival Brandon. The newspaper the day after that game had the following as part of the box score: "Multiple Hits—Ainsworth, 2." Never mind that my two hits consisted of a swinging bunt down the third base line and a popup that landed in the Bermuda Triangle among the first baseman, second baseman, and right fielder. As we say in the baseball universe, "they looked like line drives in the book."

When district play began, we found that we were as competitive as we had hoped and prepared to be. With another sterling 9-1 district record, we were once again district champs. Another common element between the '83 and '84 teams was that I played a part in the lone district loss, this time to district doormat East Flora. We shared Dennis with the track team that day, and I was penciled in the line-up as the starting right fielder that day. There's another saying in baseball that you can't hide anybody on the field on any given day. Two long fly balls (of which Dennis would likely have caught at least one) and an impotent offense led to a 2-1 defeat, our only district loss and East Flora's only district win.

Having moved up a class, we entered the South State tournament as the host team once again, as the hosting rotation for Class BB was fortuitous to the Tigers that year. Our first game against a good Clarkdale team from near Meridian was a nip-and-tuck affair that saw us advance into the winner's bracket with a one-run victory. However, in our second round game, we faced powerhouse North Forrest, who was in the midst of a three-year run as state champions, and we did not fare well. The following day, we would face Clarkdale again with a short trip to Brandon for the state tournament on the line.

Game three for us in the South State tournament was the most exciting game I was ever a part of as a player. The game was close throughout, and we entered the seventh and final inning with a slim one-run advantage. Though we were playing on our home field, Clarkdale was the home team on the scoreboard that day. With our ace, Sidney Wheatley, on the mound and cruising, our team and our fans were ready to count down the outs and advance to the state tournament. Then, something highly unusual happened. Sidney lost control of his pitches and walked the leadoff batter, then the second batter. He began to press and walked the third batter. With the bases loaded and nobody out, Sidney threw three straight balls to the next Clarkdale hitter.

Then, with the most amazing back-to-the-wall resolve I have ever seen, Sidney Wheatley threw strike one. And strike two. And with the opposing batter looking for the ball that would tie the game, he threw strike three. Sidney went on to strike out the next two batters, and the celebration that had seemed so improbable five minutes earlier finally erupted. We had punched our ticket to the state tournament. Just two years after starting a baseball program without a field, two years after not winning a game all season, the McLaurin Tigers were one of the best four baseball teams in our classification.

Our team finished the 1984 season with three consecutive losses, once more to North Forrest for the South State title and to Mooreville and Caledonia in the state tournament just up the road in Brandon. A photo in the newspaper captured my last day as a Tiger. In the photo I was, appropriately enough, getting thrown out attempting to steal third. The photographer was gracious to show the tag as a close play.

Dennis and I left a roster that had the potential for McLaurin's first state title. Talent-wise, neither of us was a major loss to the team, but we had been part of the core from the beginning. The 1985 season would indeed become the most memorable season in the school's history in so many ways; one event from that season that I have saved for the last chapter of this book would shape the rest of our lives forever.

Several of my teammates eventually went on to play college baseball, and four of us—including my brother and me—would ultimately coach at the high school level. Never, though, did any of us do anything on the baseball field that was as fulfilling as going from nothing to state title contenders. As important as I believe academics and other extra-curricular pursuits are, I also know from my experience and others that there are lessons that you only learn in sports that prepare you for life's inevitable harder lessons to come. These were lessons that the McLaurin Tiger team of 1985 would have to face all too soon.

During my years as a high school coach, I once asked a wise, more-experienced athletic director about the biggest change he had seen in high school sports during his 30-plus years as a coach. He responded quickly, "Players and parents no longer see the value in simply being part of the team."

I do, Coach...I do.

49 WORST TO FIRST ON THE COOL CAR CHART

My first car was Pop's old baby blue 1967 Mercury Capri. It was the three-speed-on-the-column tank with which I attempted to destroy the hedges across from the Star Volunteer Fire Department when I was first learning to drive. The car, with its two vinyl-covered bench seats, was plenty roomy to transport my sisters and brother and me to and from school each day. I was a junior in high school when I drove the baby blue Capri, though. I found that a roomy interior, wings, and a baby blue color did nothing to register the Capri on the cool car chart at McLaurin High School.

Since I was to be connected to the Mercury for the duration of that school year and perhaps beyond, I began to contemplate ways to lessen the blow to my standing. Though driving anything was a step above riding the bus to and from school, my car was the smallest such step. I couldn't change the enormity of my ride, and re-covering the seats seemed a little out of my league, but...Dad painted cars in his shop beside the house as a side job. Yeah, that was it; I could get the Mercury painted a cool, darker color, and my reputation could be salvaged.

I settled on a nice metallic blue somewhere between royal and navy. I helped Dad get the old car ready to paint, and he began to spray as I anxiously awaited my "new" car. After the paint had dried, we removed the paper and tape and pulled it out of the shop to find that it looked...better. Not sporty, certainly, but better. It was no Camaro or Trans Am, but at least it was no longer baby blue.

Still, the paint job only allowed me to compete for the not-quite-ugliest car on the McLaurin campus. Kenny McLain's Galaxie, though certainly sportier, was at least as big and without the new paint job. We both found comfort in one another's "sweet rides."

Between my junior and senior years, my dad decided to spruce up his old truck. He had bought the pale green short-wheel-base Ford pickup with the round hubcaps brand new in 1969. In the summer of 1983, he gave that plain truck an epic makeover: chrome rims, chrome rails, and a fresh paint job. Dad chose metallic deep-green paint with an old-gold stripe that ran down either side and across the hood—perfectly matching our school colors. I began to see the potential for my standing in the high school vehicle world undergoing as dramatic a change as Dad's truck had.

By the end of the summer of '83, I had coerced my dad into switching vehicles with me. The first day of school (finally) rolled around, and the four of us Ainsworth kids piled in the truck. The significant downgrade in roominess didn't really bother me; after all, the driver's seat was about the same. I was about to fly up the cool car chart, and I would take my sisters' and my brother's passenger reputations up with mine as a driver. They could just scrunch up and enjoy the ride, as far as I was concerned.

I had anticipated correctly that I would rise from (arguably) worst to first. My "new" truck was a hit! I felt bad for Kenny McLain, but what's a guy to do. But a funny thing continued to happen on the cool car chart that year. Tammy Mangum got a new Z-28, and then Julie Neely got a new Firebird. Then, Sidney Wheatley got a brand-new Z-28, and he was only a sophomore. Oh, well. I may have been a one-hit wonder in the cool car world, but I had my 15 minutes of fame at our high school, anyway.

From a guy who has twice now driven old Buick LeSabres handed down from my mother-in-law as my regular ride, I'll take my 15 minutes.

50 EXCEPTION TO THE BROTHER CODE

Now that I am a dad of two boys myself, I realize just how difficult it is for little brothers to be funny in the eyes of their big brothers, try though they might. I am three years older than Andy. If something was funny to me, chances are that the humor was too mature for him. And if something was funny to him, chances are the humor was too juvenile for me. That's the way brothers tend to operate if even just a few years separate them.

Maybe you didn't come from a family with brothers, so let me share a little about the brother code here. The code allows, even encourages, older brothers to make fun of and laugh *at* their little brothers. Laughing *with* them at something or someone else—in the privacy of just the brothers—is acceptable as long as that conversation is not repeated to outsiders. For an older brother to laugh at something that a little brother says that was intended to be funny in the presence of others, though...that breaks the code and just shouldn't be done. (Hey, don't roll your eyes at me; I didn't *write* the code.)

There was this one time, though, when I had to give my brother his comedic due, if for timing alone. I was probably a sophomore or junior in high school, so Andy would have been a seventh or eighth grader. My afternoons in the spring were spent at baseball practice for McLaurin High School as a light-hitting first baseman and part-time batting practice pitcher. Andy's spring afternoons were spent on the field, too, as our team manager.

One day at baseball practice, Coach Butts spent the better part of the day preventing our future public humiliation. I would later learn to call what we did that day "battlegrounds." That's where the coach hits pop up after pop up after pop up, teaching the players how to communicate with one another while simultaneously tracking the ball. We learned that day to call the ball three times: "I got it! I got it! I got it!" (bad grammar, yes, but effective for its purpose). In order to prevent collisions, any players near the player calling for the pop up were to respond, "Take it! Take it! Take it!"

In addition to the "I got its" and the "take its," we also had to learn the priority list that came into play when two players called for the ball at the same time. I remember that practice as mentally exhausting as we covered every possible pop up scenario that Coach Butts could envision. That was probably a pretty boring day for Andy since he had little to do, but we both arrived home late that afternoon ready for a good supper.

Just before supper, the phone rang. One of my sisters was evidently expecting a phone call because she sprang down the hall toward the phone with the exclamation, "I got it!!!" To which Andy instinctively responded, "Take it! Take it! Take it!" and backed away. His timing was so perfect that I must confess that I broke the code that day.

51 PROM AND MY PARENTS' PECULIAR HABIT

Mom and Dad burned most of our household trash in a 55-gallon drum behind our house. We lived out in the country where trash pick-up was something you saw on TV or read about in a book. There was a dumpster or two in Star, but it was much easier to take it out back and burn whatever could be burned. At least it was easier for everyone except my parents.

Mom and Dad did a pretty good job of sorting through the trash before it was ever taken out to the burn barrel. Leftovers were taken care of by the dogs. Vegetable peelings and the like were collected in a separate bucket and tossed between rows in the garden as organic fertilizer. Large, indestructible items like non-working lawnmowers were hauled over the hill to a gully that seemed just right to collect such things. Everything that could be burned was then burned in the trash barrel.

My parents, however, had the peculiar habit of sorting through *every single item* of trash before setting it on fire. My sisters and brother and I gave them a hard time about their poking through the trash. After all, if people wanted to keep particular items, they wouldn't have thrown them in the trash, now, would they? I would hold to this condescending view of my parents' refuse disposal habits until late into my senior year of high school.

I was preparing for my senior prom. The song "Sharp Dressed

Man" by ZZ Top was popular in 1984 and set the standard for how a young man should dress for his senior prom. My friend Ricky and I worked together to make sure we measured up, at least as much as our meager budgets would afford. On one trip to the mall, we added money clips to our list of "Sharp Dressed Man" adornments. Money, after all, looks more impressive in a money clip than it does stuffed inside some silly wallet. I proved this to my parents on my return home from the mall that night, proudly displaying my only one hundred-dollar bill in my shiny, new money clip. Oh, yeah, I *was* "all that."

A few days later, as the night of prom approached, I began to lay out my accessories. I discovered to my extreme trepidation that though my money clip was where it should have been, the hundred-dollar bill was nowhere to be found. I never remembered taking it from the clip. I tore my room apart looking for it to no avail. In my mind I retraced every step from the top of the steps above our den—the last place I knew for sure that I had seen my money—to where I had placed my money clip but no luck. One hundred dollars—gone! The prom ticket and the rented Cutlass were paid for already, but my date's corsage and our dinner weren't going to pay for themselves.

My dad offered to loan me a hundred dollars so that I wouldn't be washing dishes in the back of a restaurant while my classmates were enjoying the prom. That was quite a relief, but I computed about a week's worth of work from my part-time job at Jitney-Jungle as the price for paying off my debt. And I had a few other ideas already in place for that money that I hadn't yet made.

A day or two before the prom, Dad was out back burning trash, sorting through every single item, of course. In the process of sorting through my garbage can, he looked inside a Camelot Music bag and found—you guessed it—my hundred-dollar bill. I was ever so happy to see it. Before it ever had a chance to "burn a hole in my pocket," as my dad would often say about money that was as good as spent, that C-note was almost literally burned. My parents' much-maligned habit had saved the day, saved prom, and saved my future earnings.

I ate at the fancy Sundancer restaurant in Jackson on prom night later that week. I can't even remember what I had to eat, much less whether or not it was any good. Looking back, that's probably because I wasn't very hungry. You see, between the time my dad found my money and the time I saw it disappear for good from my money clip at the Sundancer, I had already eaten about a hundred dollars' worth of crow.

52 DOUG FLUTIE AND A LOAD OF FIREWOOD

There are certain days that you remember exactly where you were. September 11, 2001, terrorist attacks—the door of the school library at the Christian school where I taught. Earthquake during the 1989 World Series—my rented house in Charleston, Mississippi, where I had just returned from a junior high football game. Collapse of the space shuttle in 1986—my apartment in Hattiesburg, where I just returned from a morning class at the University of Southern Mississippi.

All of those are important dates in American history. November 23, 1984, was not such a date. Nevertheless, I remember where I was that day and why I was there. I recall the urgency of the morning and the steadfastness of my dad to teach his sons a valuable lesson in getting-along-ness.

I do not remember the lead-up to the morning of the 23rd. However, I have always been, by nature, an aggravator; a few months away at college had had not yet tempered this character trait (nor has the almost 30 years since. I am my father's son). Therefore, I take responsibility for what certainly must have happened on Thanksgiving afternoon and evening the previous day. My brother and I had been celebrating our break from school by arguing back and forth about who-knows-what. This was normal fare for Andy and me, but on that day, my dad had had enough. He sent us to bed with the announcement that we would be rising early on Friday morning to go deep into my grandfather's woods to cut a load of firewood.

This was devastating news to Andy and me. We had planned our weekend around the football game that would feature the #10 Boston College Eagles visiting the defending national champion and #12 Miami Hurricanes. Doug Flutie versus Bernie Kosar. David vs. Goliath. It was that week's "Game of the Century" and could not be missed by teenage college football fans. But Dad didn't budge.

The morning broke bright and crisp, a perfect day to stay inside and watch college football. Or to load up in the old, black long wheel-base Chevy truck and head to the back side of the place to serve our penance. Andy and I shuddered under several layers of clothes as Dad proceeded to fell a large pin oak. We passed the time attempting to calculate the time that would be required to cut, split, and load the firewood into the back of the old Chevy. Dad would cut the tree into the correct lengths for our wood-burning stove, I would split the wood, and Andy would load it onto the truck. We did not anticipate completing the task by kickoff, but we were hopeful to catch the second half.

We caught a break when I discovered that this pin oak was easily split-able, also the reason that the neck of the ax I was using survived that particular day (as I did not inherit my dad's pinpoint aim with an ax). We all quickly shed jackets and long-sleeve shirts as the morning moved toward noon and as the back of the truck began to fill with firewood.

When Dad finished cutting up the tree with the chain saw, he grabbed an ax and began to help me split. This, too, was an unexpected turn of events and fortuitous toward our objective. Perhaps Dad saw that Andy and I had suddenly developed an unquenchable brotherly love through his little experiment. Indeed, we were chasing the same clock with a common goal of seeing as much of the BC-Miami game as possible. Though I do recall having to remind Andy of the urgency of our task a couple of times as he grew weary, we still had hope.

When at last we emerged from the woods, Andy and I made a beeline for the television. We found that the game was still in the third quarter and that it was living up to the all the hype that had led up to it. The hype that had fueled the resolve of two teenage boys doing time deep in the Star, Mississippi, woods and cut off from all media. When Doug Flutie faded back with six seconds to go and his team trailing 45-41, he never knew the price we had paid to see it. With our muscles twitching from unexpected but deserved overuse, Gerard Phelan fell between two Miami defenders, clutching the ball to his chest in the Hurricanes' end zone. Touchdown Boston College.

I have seen that miracle pass and catch replayed hundreds of times since then as one of the all-time great plays in college football history. Each time I see it, I remember that Al and Andy Ainsworth—with yeomen's effort—had seen it live, never to forget the game or the lesson attached to it.

53 REMEMBERING MIKE

I finished high school on top of the world. I graduated with top honors and played in the baseball state tournament a week later. One of my graduation gifts was the first car that I could ever completely call mine, a 1973 Comet GT. I had earned a nice scholarship to the University of Southern Mississippi, my school of choice. I was all set.

I have only recently been able to piece together how my world began to crumble in the fall of '84. During the summer before my freshman year began, I began to attend parties hosted by various USM fraternities. I already knew which one I would pledge, but I checked out the others, too. I couldn't have been more out of my comfort zone, and I couldn't have had less in common with the "brothers" with whom I spent most of my time for the next few months. I had had my first taste of alcohol as a high school senior and had experimented with it more than I would like to admit. During that first semester at Southern Miss, though, alcohol became my increasingly present companion.

Only after years of hindsight did I realize just how badly I felt the need to fit in somewhere. Baseball was over for me; I knew that, but I didn't appreciate the depth of the bonds I had made on my high school team, striving for a common goal and enjoying the camaraderie that comes with that.

I returned to school in January 1985 for the second semester of my freshman year with a resolution to make some changes. Only a couple of weeks after my return to Hattiesburg, I realized just how little I had in common with my fraternity brothers if I removed alcohol from the equation, which I had done upon my return to school. Under the threat of financial retribution, I quit my fraternity and began to meet some guys who would be my friends for free.

I returned home for spring break of 1985 and spent a sizable amount of it following my old high school baseball teammates as they competed against the best talent in the Jackson area. I still felt a part of the program that I had helped build, and spring break that year may have been the best part of my freshman year of college.

Aside from the games, I spent a great deal of time with Mike Abel that week. "Deadeye" was a newcomer on the team my senior year, but he fit in as if he had been around since the beginning of the baseball program my sophomore year. All my teammates would concur that he never seemed younger than us.

School started back, and I still talked to Mike regularly as he kept me updated on the progress of the team. On Monday night, April 1, I talked to Mike for about 45 minutes, and he informed me that the upset of the century was taking place in the national championship basketball game. Georgetown had been so heavily favored over Villanova that I hadn't even bothered to watch the game. Mike sent me off to watch the second half of one of the greatest upsets in college basketball history, and we promised to talk the following day when McLaurin would play their first district baseball game.

On April 2, I was sitting in my dorm room late in the afternoon, and my phone rang. Beth, one of my high school classmates who also attended Southern Miss, was on the line. We had not talked much since arriving on campus, so this phone call was unusual.

"Al, have you heard the news from McLaurin today?" she asked.

Oh no, I thought. I could tell by the tone of her voice that this was not good news. They lost their first district game today, I surmised. That's okay, we had lost one in each of the last two years and still won district. They would be okay.

"Al," Beth said, reminding me that she was still on the line, "Mike Abel had a seizure or something like that on the baseball field today."

I had just begun to process what her words meant when she followed with the bombshell, "And, Al, he didn't make it."

Those words have now hung suspended for almost 30 years. No, it couldn't be! Not Mike. I just talked to him last night. I just spent time with him two weeks ago. He was there. He was real. NO!

I made my way through the line at the funeral home the following night, still in stunned disbelief. After going through the motions of paying my respects to Mike's family like it was still just a bad dream, I had to walk outside to catch my breath. I remember one of my former teammates—I can't even tell you which one— putting his hand on my shoulder and telling me that I had to let it go...the grief, that is. As I had done the night before, I cried long and hard. I swapped Deadeye stories with my teammates, and we laughed a little and cried a lot more.

I made my way to my friend Steven's house that night, where his mom answered many questions that I had about death and eternity. I don't remember a single question I asked her or a single one of her answers, just that my curiosity was satisfied, and I was ready to make the seemingly long drive back to my parents' house.

Somewhere between Shell Oil Road and what would soon become Ainsworth Road, I made my peace with God. My own mortality had become evident, and I confessed that I did not have what it took to be in control of my own life, and I asked Him to take over. I may not have said the words exactly like I would later learn as the language of salvation, but that night Jesus became Lord of my life.

On April 2, 1985, Mike Abel passed away from a heart attack on the field that now bears his name. I think that much of what was left of my childhood came to a stop on that day. On April 3, 1985, I was reborn into God's family. The two events will forever be tied together, inextricably joined together as the worst and best moments of my life.

My son Drew bears Mike's name as his middle name. I certainly don't need the reminder of who Mike Abel was and how special his memory is to me. People for generations to come, though, will ask Drew Michael Ainsworth about the origin of his name. The legacy of my friendship with Mike and the legacy of the work that God has done in my life will live on every time he tells...and re-tells that story.

My former high school teammates played valiantly through their pain for the rest of the 1985 season, landing a berth in the state championship tournament but falling a few wins short of a title. Though none of my teammates ever won a state championship, we had laid the groundwork for something special. In the spring of 1991, in just its 10th season as a high school baseball program and six years after Mike's passing, McLaurin High School won the Mississippi Class AA State Championship. I was in the first base dugout as the players piled onto Mike Abel Field to celebrate.

I just stood there and remembered. And smiled.

CONCLUSION

Except for a few skirmishes with peer pressure (that somehow didn't manage to ruin my life), the conflict of my life's story pales in comparison with the life stories of many others. Does that mean my story shouldn't have been written? I certainly hope that's not the case because the process of writing this portion of my story wasn't an easy one.

Writing some of the stories originally as blog posts on my site at www.familystorylegacy.com gave me some early momentum and encouragement, but compiling the stories and writing them one by one has been like writing 53 separate short stories (plus an introduction and this conclusion). Each had its own prologue, conflict, and resolution. Each writing day essentially required starting the writing process all over again.

Writing the stories was not the most difficult part of developing the book, though. The stories were fun to write, and the writing process has solidified both fond and difficult memories in my mind. However, a bigger question loomed over me for many months. I didn't believe that my desire to write a memoir had just suddenly manifested in my life like some latent passion that had been lying dormant for years.

My desire was to reach a bigger audience with a broader message than just my family's collection of stories. I believed the purpose of the book was greater than nostalgia. I contemplated the various aspects of this idea. I even prayed and asked God why He had given me this particular desire.

One day last fall, I was blowing leaves out of the flowerbeds in my backyard. While mindlessly completing this chore, the answer to the purpose behind *Lines in the Gravel (and 52 Other Re-Told Childhood Tales)* came to me like this: ***Nostalgia reaches into the past with both hands to grasp something that is already gone and likely never will be again. Legacy, on the other hand, reaches into the past with one hand to grasp what is teachable and passes it forward with the other hand to the next generation.*** Yes, that was it!

I have had three distinct career callings before this season as a writer and speaker. As a coach, a teacher, and a pastor, I have spent the better part of my life preparing people for next stages in their lives. That looked different in each role, but the principle of legacy building was consistent through it all. You see, like it or not, we all represent much more than just ourselves. I didn't coach to just try to win games but to pass on an appreciation for competition and sportsmanship. As an English teacher, I swam upstream against pop culture to teach an appreciation for classic literature. As a pastor I urged those in my circle of influence to live with an understanding and an appreciation of the high price that many have paid throughout the generations for the gospel to reach our generation. In all three roles, I called for more than a simple token look at the past in preparation for those under my influence to positively impact the future.

I believe every person plays a key role in his generation. No matter what hand you have been dealt by your genealogy, I believe your role in your place in time is critical. You may be the one whose task is to pass on values that have already been handed down for generations in your family. If that's the case, you're not going to be the one to break that chain, are you?

I know other people from families like mine who are as close to what you would call "normal" as you can imagine. They come from healthy families. The world needs folks like us who can point the way for others who want to leave a legacy of strong family values. We can't drop the ball in our generation and expect someone else to pick it up on down the line.

Maybe you have inherited quite a bit of "not-so-normal" from the generations before you. Ahhhh, you are in quite a heroic position, though you may not realize it yet. You can choose to be a champion to succeeding generations by doing the work to break the grip of generational dysfunction. Yes, that's difficult. No, you may never get proper credit for it. But generations later, your family tree will be more healthy because of you.

I have friends who can look back at major strongholds in their family histories—alcoholism, broken marriages, racism, greed, drug abuse, and so many more. Many of them can look back at particular people who changed their families' trajectories. Some of my friends are the ones working to make this change. Their lives can be a mess as they work toward the future, but they are my heroes. They are living for more than themselves. They are living for a blessing they may never fully realize in their lifetimes.

Whether you come from a "functional" family or one that struggled, I believe that the best vehicle for passing down values from one generation to the next is story. The stories that we tell...and re-tell are important well past their entertainment value; they can serve as vehicles for values. Let's say, for example, that you want to instill a strong work ethic in others, whether that's in a family or organizational setting. What stories can you tell about your acquiring a strong work ethic? Or maybe you can tell stories of opportunities you may have missed because you didn't work hard enough. Either way, people remember stories, and within them, values are communicated.

I hope that you have enjoyed the hijinks and highlights of my childhood as I have told them through the stories in this book. These are the stories that my family tells...and re-tells when we get together for any length of time. I have intentionally not lectured you about the values that are most important to us, but...I bet you could easily make a list of the ideals that we treasure most and from where we formed them.

Intentionally attaching values to the stories we tell is what I call values storying. What are the values that you want to pass along to another generation of family (or students or employees)? Think about the stories that could enhance your communication of those values. Maybe you should collect them and publish them, and maybe you should just tell your stories out loud. Whichever works best for you, I challenge you to begin to tell...and re-tell those stories over time in order to impact the next generation for good.

BONUS CHAPTER FROM *ABBOISMS (AND OTHER SUCH SAMUNCRIUM)* (COMING SOON)

YOU THOUGHT LIKE PARKER'S DOG

I remember as a kid seeing a VFW sign and asking my dad what VFW stood for. He replied, "Volunteer Fire Women." Okay, so then I knew. Only, VFW really stands for Veterans of Foreign Wars.

I grew up in Star, Mississippi. I can be a shade on the naive side. We had a volunteer fire department in Star, so I didn't consider it outside the realm of possibility that the wives of the volunteer firefighters might gather for some refreshments and fellowship on the night the volunteer firemen had their meeting. Right? Well, what would you have thought?

Unfortunately, that was not the only time I would fall prey to my Dad's sense of humor....

There was this church, Christian Fellowship M.B. Church, that sat adjacent to our church. One day, I became curious about the M.B. in their sign and in others I had seen, so I asked my dad what M.B. stood for. He answered, "Mostly black." Okay, so then I knew. Only, M.B. stands for Missionary Baptist. Well, all the people I had seen coming and going from the church were black, so it made sense at the time. As I noticed the other M.B. churches in our area, I thought I knew what they were. Only, I didn't really. Dad would say that I "thought like Parker's dog."

My naivety turned around and laughed at me when I asked my dad about Parker's dog. Any time I would excuse a thought or behavior by saying, "But I thought...," Dad would answer, "You thought like Parker's dog." Years passed, and I never thought to ask the obvious question. I just thought that "you thought like Parker's dog" was something every family said to identify a false assumption. It never occurred to me that this saying was peculiar to our family.

I just thought Dad knew someone named Parker who had a dog who wasn't so bright (kind of like my uncle's dog, Booger Red, that I wrote about in *Lines in the Gravel*). When it finally occurred to me to ask about Parker's dog, though, I asked the wrong question. I asked Dad who this Parker was. Wrong direction. The correct question would have been what Parker's dog thought. Ready for this?

Parker's dog thought—shall we say—that he was eating a chocolate biscuit. (Or to be perfectly accurate in quoting my dad, "He thought doodoo was a biscuit and he ate it.")

So then I knew. And now you know.

ABOUT THE AUTHOR

Al Ainsworth is a writer and speaker who focuses on "values storying," the use of the vehicle of story to pass along values to the next generation—whether the next generation of family, employees, students, or church members. Through careers in teaching, coaching, and pastoring, he has prepared others for the next phases of their lives through the values that he often relates through his unique style of storytelling.

Al lives with his wife, Loretta, and their three children—Ashton, Garrett, and Drew—in Hernando, Mississippi.

∎∎∎

Al blogs regularly at www.familystorylegacy.com.

Contact him through his speaker's page at www.alainsworth.com.

∎∎∎

Made in the USA
Charleston, SC
22 April 2014